T H E
C O R O N E T
T H E A T R E

T0352777

THE

LODGER

by Robert Holman

The Lodger was first performed on 10 September 2021 at
The Coronet Theatre, Notting Hill, London.

THE LODGER

by Robert Holman

CAST

Esther	Penny Downie
Dolly	Sylvestra Le Touzel
Jude	Matthew Tennyson
Anila	Iniki Mariano

CREATIVE TEAM

Director	Geraldine Alexander
Set and Costume Designer	Richard Kent
Lighting Designer	David Plater
Composer and Sound Designer	Simon Slater
Casting Director	Katie Mozumder

PRODUCTION TEAM

Head of Production	Andy McDonald
Associate Production Manager	Jack Boissieux
Company Stage Manager	Emma Smith
Assistant Stage Manager	Alexandra Kettell
Chief Electrician	Alex Ramsden
Production Sound Engineer	Jack Baxter
Costume Supervisor	Lisa Aitkin
Dialect Coach	Jessica Dennis
Production Photography	Tristram Kenton
Graphic Design	North

CREATIVES

Robert Holman *Playwright*
Robert Holman writes plays of startling beauty, combining close observation of the way people behave with a thrilling and often fiercely uncompromising mastery of dramatic form. He is the playwright most admired by other playwrights. To Simon Stephens, he is 'My favourite living writer.'

His work has been produced since the 1970s at the RSC, the West End, Royal Court Theatre and elsewhere in the UK. His plays include *The Natural Cause*; *Mud*; *Outside the Whale*; *German Skerries* (for which he won the George Devine Award); *Other Worlds*; *Today*; *The Overgrown Path*; *Making Noise Quietly*; *Across Oka*; *Rafts and Dreams*; *Bad Weather*; *Holes in the Skin*; and *Jonah and Otto*.

Geraldine Alexander *Director*
For The Coronet, Geraldine directed *Deathwatch* by Genet adapted by David Rudkin, her play; *Amygdala* and workshops on her adaptation of *The Book and The Brotherhood* by Iris Murdoch and *A Secret Play* by Ben Okri. For the Storyhouse in Chester she directed a 'shatteringly powerful production' of *The Crucible* by Arthur Miller. For the RSC festival she directed Tabori's *Wisemen and Copperface*. Amongst her many productions at RADA she recently directed Shakespeare's *Richard III*, *Broadway Bound* by Neil Simon and Thornton Wilder's *Our Town*. Over lockdown she co-founded a company for recent drama graduates and after a year of weekly Zoom rehearsals they had their first live performance of *Citizens' Richard* in June 2021. Geraldine is also an actress and writer, who has appeared widely on stage and screen and is currently on screen in *Bridgerton*, *The One* and *Oslo*.

Richard Kent *Set and Costume Designer*
Richard Kent trained at the Liverpool Institute for Performing Arts (2004–2007) and was awarded the Phillip Holt Trust Commendation Award on graduation. Recent credits include: *When The Crows Visit* (Kiln Theatre); *The Mirror Crack'd* (Wales Millennium Centre); *Handbagged* (Round House Theatre – Washington); *Disco Pigs* (The Irish Repertory Theatre – New York/Tara Finney Productions); *Heroin* (HighTide/Theatr Clwyd); *The Winter's Tale* (Shakespeare's Globe); *Richard II* (Donmar Warehouse); *Le Nozze Di Figaro* (Glyndebourne Festival Opera); *Don Giovanni* (Metropolitan Opera House, New York); *Madame Butterfly* (Houston Grand Opera).

David Plater *Lighting Designer*
David Plater trained at RADA. He spent seventeen years at the Donmar Warehouse where he was Head of Lighting. His nominations include: Olivier, Tony, Drama Desk nominee for Best Lighting Design for *Bring Up The Bodies* (Winter Garden Theatre, Broadway & Aldwych West End); Knight of Illumination Award for *Richard II* (Best Play Lighting) in 2012 and for *This is My Family* (Best Musical Lighting) in 2013. Recent credits include: *Musik* (Leicester Square Theatre); *This is My Family* (Chichester Festival Theatre); *My Cousin Rachel* (Theatre Royal Bath); *Porgy & Bess* (Grange Park Opera); *The Outsider* (The Print Room); *Approaching Empty* (Tamasha Theatre Company); *Ballet Black 2018* (Ballet Black); *Misalliance* (Orange Tree Theatre); *Room* (Theatre Royal Stratford East); *The Mentalists* (Wyndham's Theatre); *The Effect* (Sheffield Theatres); *Richard III* & *Twelfth Night* (Shakespeare's Globe/Apollo Theatre).

Simon Slater *Composer and Sound Designer*
Simon Slater is an award-winning composer of over 300 original scores for theatre, film, television and radio. Recent credits include: *The Winter's Tale* (Shakespeare's Globe); *Carmen Disruption* (Almeida Theatre); *The BFG* (Octagon Bolton); *The Doll's House* (Sherman Cardiff); *Alice in Wonderland* (Watermill Theatre); *Octagon* (Arcola Theatre); *Constellations* (New York/Manhattan Theatre); *The Father* (Trafalgar Studios); *Single Spies* (Rose Theatre, Kingston); *Wonderland* (Hampstead Theatre); *Sleeping Beauty* (Theatre Royal Winchester); *A Handful of Stars* (Theatre503/Trafalgar Studios); *Ghosts* (New Vic Stoke); *Foreplay* (King's Head).

Katie Mozumder *Casting Director*
Katie Mozumder worked in television production before moving to casting, working as a freelance assistant for Kate Rhodes James, Jina Jay, Sasha Robertson & Sarah Trevis. Since 2017 Katie has been working for Casting Directors Suzanne Crowley & Gilly Poole on a wide range of television projects for BBC America, ITV, UKTV and Sky. Katie has also assisted casting for several theatre projects for Hampstead Theatre and most recently *The Sunset Limited* at the Boulevard Theatre, directed by Terry Johnson.

CAST

Penny Downie *Esther*
Penny Downie began her career in Australia, later joining the Royal Shakespeare Company. Among her many appearances were Gertrude in the acclaimed 2009 *Hamlet*, Hermione/Perdita in *The Winter's Tale*, and the title role in Margaret Atwood's *The Penelopiad*. She received the Peggy Ashcroft Award for her Portia.

For the National Theatre she has appeared as Chorus in *Henry V*, Katherine in *Enemy of the People*, and Wynne in *Dinner*, among many other roles.

Her most recent stage appearances include *Helen* (Shakespeare's Globe); *Ghosts* (Royal & Derngate); *Rabbit Hole* (Hampstead Theatre); *The Fairy Queen* (Glyndebourne); *Judgement Day* (The Print Room); and *Butley* (Duchess Theatre).

Penny has worked extensively in TV, notably as the Duchess of Gloucester in *The Crown* and as Lady Sinderby in *Downton Abbey*. She recently reprised her role of Ellen in the Channel 4 comedy *Back*.

Film work includes *Invictus, Breathe, Jackie, London Has Fallen, Crime and Punishment*.

Sylvestra Le Touzel *Dolly*
Sylvestra Le Touzel is a British television, film and stage actor.

Her most recent TV appearances include *Intelligence, Roadkill, The Crown, Endeavour, Big School, Father Brown, Appropriate Adult* and in film, *The Death of Stalin, Radioactive, Mr Turner* and *Cloud Atlas*.

Sylvestra has recently taken part in many theatre productions including *Alys, Always* (Bridge Theatre); *Hogarth's Progress* (Rose Theatre); *The Pride of Miss Jean Brodie* (Donmar Warehouse); *Giving* (Hampstead Theatre); *Waste* (National Theatre); *The Audience* (Playful Productions); *Merry Wives of Windsor* (RSC); *Les Parents Terribles* (Donmar Warehouse); *Ivanov* (Donmar Warehouse).

Matthew Tennyson *Jude*

Theatre: *A Monster Calls* (The Old Vic/Bristol Old Vic); *Salomé* (Royal Shakespeare Company); *Cleansed* (National Theatre); *The Seagull* (Regent's Park Open Air Theatre); *A Breakfast of Eels* (The Coronet Theatre); *A Midsummer Night's Dream* (Shakespeare's Globe); *Making Noise Quietly* (Donmar Warehouse); *Beautiful Thing* (Manchester Royal Exchange); *Flare Path* (Theatre Royal Haymarket). Television: *A Midsummer Night's Dream, Grantchester, Borgia, Humans, Babylon, Father Brown, The Hollow Crown*. Film: *Benediction, Making Noise Quietly, Pride*.

Iniki Mariano *Anila*

Iniki was born and raised in Singapore where she made her television and stage debuts. She trained at the Guildhall School of Music and Drama in London where she now resides. Recent stage credits include Sally Cookson's *Peter Pan* (National Theatre/BOV); 'Mowgli' in *The Jungle Book* (Derby Theatre); *Can't Wait for Christmas!* (Orange Tree Theatre). Film includes *The Retreat* by Marcus Anthony Thomas, available on *Short of the Week*. You can see her COVID project *Me... Me* on virtualcollaborators.co.uk

Iniki would like to dedicate this performance to her family, Nana and Gloria.

THE CORONET THEATRE

The Coronet Theatre is a risk-taking, international theatre in an iconic, Grade II listed building in London's Notting Hill. Both its programme and the building's restoration is curated by Artistic Director & CEO Anda Winters.

The Coronet Theatre presents an eclectic programme of theatre, film, dance, music, poetry and visual art in its intimate 195-seat main auditorium and 90-seat studio space, re-named The Print Room in recognition of the company's previous home at a nearby print works.

A fusion of multi-disciplinary international and UK work, The Coronet Theatre stages a mix of new productions, commissions and visiting artists, including a number of UK and world premieres. We offer memorable and often unexpected experiences for our audiences, while supporting established artists and nurturing new talent.

103 Notting Hill Gate
London W11 3LB

thecoronettheatre.com
020 3642 6606

We are a registered charity no. 1141921

SUPPORT US

The Coronet Theatre is a theatre unlike any other.

Our programme is an eclectic fusion of theatre, poetry, dance, music and visual art from both emerging and established artists.

Our productions give audiences the chance to see the best international talent in a uniquely intimate setting.

Our building has a rich history that we must preserve and share with visitors from Notting Hill and beyond.

The past year has presented an extraordinary challenge to our Theatre. Now more than ever, The Coronet Theatre needs your help to maintain the accessibility, diversity and excellence of our exceptional artistic programme.

Support our mission by making a donation, joining us as a Patron member, or becoming a corporate donor, and then enjoy our variety of fantastic benefits. Every donation counts and makes a massive difference.

To find out more please contact the Development team:

020 8051 0466

giving@thecoronettheatre.com
www.thecoronettheatre.com/support-us

We would like to thank all of our Patrons and donors for their support towards our work.

THE LODGER

Robert Holman

Characters

JUDE TWELVETREES, *Esther's lodger, twenties*
ESTHER, *a teacher and novelist, sixties*
DOLLY WARBURTON, *Esther's older sister, a housewife*
ANILA, *a student, early twenties*

The play takes place in Little Venice in London, in Dungeness, and Lake Tyrifjorden in Norway.

There is an interval between Acts One and Two.

This text went to press before the end of rehearsals and so may differ slightly from the play as performed.

ACT ONE

Scene One

*A spacious utility room in the basement of a flat (on two floors)
in Little Venice. A July day, after midnight. There is a big,
shuttered window and a door close by, both open to let in the
air. The traffic sounds of London come into the room too easily
through the heat of the night. Outside are metal steps down
from the street above, and a yellow street light. A washing
machine on the dry cycle. An old cooker and a new fridge.
A square sink with old taps. A new boiler. A sideboard and a
wardrobe with a broken door. A good oak table, chairs, and the
paraphernalia of lives lived. There are pictures on the walls and
rugs on the floor.*

JUDE, *a young man in his twenties, is on the sofa. He is
throwing darts at a dartboard on the wall some distance away.
Most of the darts miss and hit the wall or simply land on the
floor. There are hundreds of them and many marks splintered in
the wood.* ESTHER, *in her sixties, comes down the steps
outside and into the room. She has a bunch of red flowers. She
switches on the light. She puts the flowers on the table and
starts to deal with them.*

ESTHER. I haven't seen you for a day or two.

JUDE. I'm here now. Is there a problem?

ESTHER. I went for a walk along the canal on the hottest
evening of the year. The air is about to burst. (*She smells one
of the blooms.*) I hope it was legal.

JUDE. I'm as honest as Jesus. Would I ever be anything else?

ESTHER. When did growing cannabis in a pot plant become a
good idea? (*She finds scissors to cut the stems.*) We'd go
along to the old cricket pavilion, tumbled down with nails
sticking up, to smoke dried banana skins and make believe
we were marrying The Beatles, in my case John. Be careful.
I'm always more cunning than I need to be.

JUDE (*he throws a dart. He sits up*). The twenty-four-hour shop closes at eleven so you can't have got them there.

ESTHER. What?

JUDE. The flowers, they're beautiful.

ESTHER. A forgetful soul put them down by a bench on the towpath and left them there, like we frequently misplace umbrellas.

JUDE. It's not like you.

ESTHER. What's not like me?

JUDE. To pick up something that doesn't belong to you. It's such a servant thing to do.

ESTHER. At this second, I'd be happy to be a servant.

JUDE. If you'd ever been a servant you'd soon change your mind.

ESTHER. It's a splendid thing to have no responsibilities, I imagine.

JUDE (*he gets to his feet*). What's the matter?

ESTHER. Jude, since I've just come in, I've obviously been out.

JUDE. I didn't ask you about that.

ESTHER. The canal is a good place to think from time to time. Be useful and find me a vase.

JUDE *takes a vase from the cupboard near the sink and takes it to the table.*

It might be more helpful if you'd think to put water in it.

JUDE. Something is wrong, and I'm not happy about it.

ESTHER. My mother died last night in the small hours of the morning.

They are both still.

The old witch has gone, she's finally popped her clogs.

JUDE. I've two ears, I can listen.

ESTHER. It's why finding these flowers has been so timely and fortuitous because every day there were new flowers about the house. There have been many times I've wanted a garden to grow shrubs, and flowers. It's the only thing we had in common. She certainly couldn't write a book, although I think, when she was a girl, she did write letters to my father. Or teach a class, she couldn't do that. She did needlecraft until her fingers were too slow. Have I said this to you before?

JUDE. No.

ESTHER. I'm sure I have.

JUDE. No, never. Esther, you've not told me this before.

ESTHER. I know I say odd little things over and again as if for the first time, but only to people I care about. I can count those people on the fingers of less than one hand. My mother was a Harrogate woman in every way, which won't mean much to you, since you're a London boy. This city has your skin. I'm a Harrogate girl. I've had these rooms in Little Venice for half a century, but London still isn't in me. My home town was too genteel, which wasn't to my taste. As a young girl I wanted to spit on some of it. My mother was the wife of a GP and that's the life she lived. She did her best to make every day a Sunday afternoon, and don't ever say what you think. A vaginaless life for ninety-eight years. I taught myself to be unpleasant. To be rude was a way to grow up, or so it seemed then. I didn't love my mother, but I didn't not love her either. I'm conflicted at this moment. My head is jumping hither and thither, which is not like me at all, as you know.

JUDE (*he points to a flower*). This one's dead.

ESTHER. Where?

JUDE. There. I've never seen you like this before.

ESTHER (*she takes out the flower*). I've not seen myself like this before.

JUDE. And another one here.

ESTHER. Yes.

JUDE. You're not yourself.

ESTHER (*she deals with the flower*). One of the canal-boat crowd has just asked me where you were.

JUDE. Who?

ESTHER. I don't know who. A few minutes ago.

JUDE. There's nothing poisonous in somebody saying hello on the canal. I should open a bottle of wine and we can both get drunk as soggy biscuits.

ESTHER. She knew who I was and even my name. We go for a walk and in our heads we're invisible, like a child who thinks she can't be seen if she shuts her eyes.

JUDE (*he takes the vase to the sink*). I'm anonymous.

ESTHER. Are you?

JUDE (*he fills the vase with water*). I know who's behind and who's in front of me.

ESTHER. Do you?

JUDE. Yes.

ESTHER. I'm obviously not as anonymous as you.

JUDE. No.

ESTHER. I only wish I was.

JUDE (*he puts the vase on the table*). You don't wish that.

ESTHER. I think I do.

JUDE. You would hate to be anonymous, it would make you ordinary.

ESTHER (*she arranges the flowers*). You're being truthful today.

JUDE. The boy in the top flat goes into a bookshop and sees your picture on a cover, and he's speechless. And you think it's wonderful he's so tongue-tied that he he he he stammers. I remember you taking me to a bookshop in Primrose Hill. You wore a funny hat as a disguise.

ESTHER. He's seventeen, so I gave him the books for his birthday in a pile.

JUDE. He's a lucky boy.

ESTHER. I gave them to you, but Buster read them, and found
the courage to ask me a hundred pointless questions about
characters I can't remember writing. I did my best to be
a friend and not to be a teacher, but I got short-tempered.

JUDE. I want to see the silly you.

The phone rings loudly.

ESTHER. Leave it. It's my sister Dolly. She's been ringing
every hour on the hour for the last twelve hours.

JUDE. The infamous sister Dolly.

ESTHER. Why is she infamous?

JUDE. The elusive sister Dolly.

ESTHER. You're being quite silly.

JUDE. I've not met her.

ESTHER. I know.

JUDE. Something weird is telling me I'm about to meet your
family.

ESTHER. Yes.

JUDE. What a crazy thing.

ESTHER. She's on her way down from Harrogate in the car.
Would you mind running the vacuum cleaner across the
floor.

JUDE. I could eat my dinner off it.

ESTHER. She'll arrive like a gale because she always does, and
criticise what she sees.

JUDE (*he goes to the wardrobe*). It's a mad thing. I knew this
morning something was wrong. I saw the day. (*He takes the
vacuum cleaner from the wardrobe*.) You are worrying far
too much.

ESTHER. Am I?

JUDE. I know about worrying, it's in my blood.

He plugs in the vacuum cleaner and turns it on. ESTHER *takes the rubbish from the flowers to the bin.*

You should go and change.

ESTHER. I should do what?

JUDE. Go and change, put on something brighter, you look dowdy.

ESTHER (*she motions to him to turn off the vacuum*). Do I look everso dowdy?

JUDE. Put on something colourful.

ESTHER. She might be a little while yet.

JUDE. That was her ringing to say she's here.

ESTHER. Yes. (*She puts the flowers in the centre of the table.*) I'm feeling vulnerable.

JUDE. I can tell.

ESTHER *opens the door to the rest of the apartment and goes upstairs.* JUDE *goes to the sink and is immediately sick into it.* DOLLY, *the older of the sisters, comes down the steps outside and stops at the door.* JUDE *turns on the tap to clear away the mess that has come out of his body. He senses someone is there, and turns.*

You must be Esther's sister Dolly.

DOLLY. For a moment I thought I'd come down the wrong steps, and who might I ask, young man, are you?

JUDE. That's for me to know and you to find out. I'm nobody. If I stand sideways I disappear. I'm not important at all.

DOLLY. You're important to somebody, it's just a matter of finding them. Where's Esther?

JUDE. She's upstairs, she's putting on a skirt.

DOLLY. Why the dickens is she doing that at this time?

JUDE. She might feel silly with nothing on and the door open.

DOLLY. If you're not a burglar, which I'm presuming you're not, then you must be one of her many hundreds of students from the university college.

JUDE. I think of myself as the lodger. I think that's what I am, a little bit more, a little bit less.

He bends down to see if clothes are dry in the washing machine.

DOLLY. Will she be very long putting on a skirt?

She sniffs the flowers.

Have I done something wrong? I've been here less than a minute and already I feel guilty. I'm getting the sense you have knowledge of me that I don't have of you, which is always unfair. I've come two hundred miles with only one toilet stop in a car with wonky gears I discover hurtling towards Peterborough.

ESTHER *comes into the room, wearing something brighter.*

Esther, dear, there you are, I was just beginning to wonder if I would ever see you again. You're looking old, but then it has been a long time.

ESTHER. I thought as the years went by I was getting younger, but obviously not.

The sisters kiss on both cheeks. DOLLY *takes an apple from her pocket.*

DOLLY. I brought you an apple. (*She puts it on the table.*) I'll put it there for you. You might like it later or in the morning. I wonder if the student would fetch my bags from the car. I've left it parked on a double-yellow but who cares. Esther dear, you've not decorated anything. If you'd told me, I'd have filled the boot with paint from our garage.

ESTHER. The car won't hurt for a minute or two at this time of night.

JUDE *looks at the washing. He takes a shirt from the machine and folds it.*

My sister is Dolly because she had twenty-three dolls as a child. It could be any number, because a new one would appear as if by magic. When we were little girls we shared a bedroom. The dolls meant the room was not mine. Today she has well over a thousand dolls from around the world, in a room of their own. Jude is not a servant.

DOLLY. Yes, of course, Esther dear.

ESTHER. Don't put him in one of your neat pigeonholes. It's not for you to decide who he is. He comes and goes as he pleases.

DOLLY. I stand corrected. (*She turns to* JUDE.) You'll find that about Esther and me, we stand corrected quite often. Or I do. If you would like the apple, please take it. I brought it to eat in the car. (*She points.*) There's a cobweb. If you point your nozzle, you'll be able to get it. Esther was clever at essays but not at dusting.

JUDE *turns on the vacuum to get the cobweb.*

I'd like a whisky if you have it.

ESTHER. I gave up whisky quite a few years ago, even when you were here the last time, like I stopped smoking.

DOLLY. A cup of tea, if you please.

JUDE *turns off the vacuum.*

Thank you, Jude.

He fills the kettle. ESTHER *goes to the sideboard to put away some crockery that is there. A chipped plate goes in the bin.*

ESTHER. Why are you wearing a coat?

DOLLY (*taking it off and putting it over a chair*). It was colder in Yorkshire. Goodness only knows why. I left in a tizzy. (*She looks at* JUDE *who is doing the tea.*) Not too strong for me, with plenty of milk. I'm at the milky-drink age. (*She looks at her sister.*) I just grabbed a coat, any coat, even though I didn't need it. It came out of the charity-shop bag. We've always one of those on the go. You can have it. And the traffic was crazy. It's a miracle I'm here in one piece. (*She turns to* JUDE.) If you've English tea that would be lovely. (*She looks at her sister.*) You've never looked good since I used to dress you.

ESTHER. Thank you, Dolly.

DOLLY. I treated you like a doll and I know that was wrong of me, thinking about it now.

ESTHER. It's far too long ago for it still to be important.

DOLLY. We don't see each other often enough. I don't know why you've been so reluctant to come north?

ESTHER. I've been to Harrogate too often, Dolly. It's a memory, it doesn't need me.

DOLLY. I think Mummy needed her daughters. We would always like to see more of you.

ESTHER. I'm sorry she's died.

DOLLY. We all are. (*She looks at her sister.*) I've wanted you by my side these last weeks with Mummy ailing in hospital. It would have been good if you'd been there to take a turn by her bed. Mummy asked to see you. If you didn't want to do the drive, it's three hours on a train. I will stay in a hotel if it would be easier for us both.

ESTHER. I've told you, you're welcome here any time.

DOLLY. Yes, and I've stayed for a few days now and again but always with the feeling I should be somewhere else. It's fifteen years since I've been here, and I think that says a lot.

JUDE (*head in the cupboard*). Teacups or mugs?

ESTHER. Dolly, a teacup or a mug?

DOLLY. An old-fashioned cup and saucer would be the highlight of my day, thank you, Jude.

ESTHER *helps* JUDE *take cups and saucers from the cupboard, and teaspoons from a drawer in the table.*

ESTHER. Jude will carry your bags from the car when he moves it. (*She takes milk from the fridge.*) I am very sorry, Dolly. I know how you've taken on every single responsibility with Mum in these last years, but it was your choice and I didn't ask you to. I did come north a month or two ago.

DOLLY. Six months for a few hours. She went to sleep and didn't wake up. If we must die, it was the best way. I saw to Mummy before I left with a good and reliable undertaker, but I couldn't stay up there, Esther dear, I know you'll understand. The flowers are enchanting. Did you get them to remember Mummy?

ESTHER. Yes, I did.

DOLLY. Mummy and I shared certain things. It's part of our sadness, Esther, that I'm like her in so many ways, and you are not like her at all.

JUDE is making the tea.

I see you still have real tea. What's wrong with a teabag? Jude, you're determined to make me feel special. (*She kicks off her shoes.*) These shoes have been killing me since Leicester.

ESTHER stirs the tea in the teapot. JUDE puts milk in the cups.

We're on our own, Esther darling. We're orphans, with only each other. It's all so terribly new.

ESTHER. It brings it home to us that we're next.

DOLLY. She didn't ask about you in the last hours.

ESTHER. I know you're angry.

DOLLY. I think she'd forgotten she had two daughters. I had to be there for both of us.

ESTHER. You didn't have to be there for me, Dolly.

She pours tea into the cups using a tea strainer.

DOLLY (*she looks at JUDE*). Esther went to the grammar school, which made her bright as a button but not always sympathetic. (*She takes in her sister.*) I'm sorry I couldn't help you with your homework. Daddy was the only one who could do that and talk philosophies at the dinner table.

ESTHER. This is just about the most ridiculous conversation I've ever had.

JUDE (*he raises his teacup*). Cheers.

They drink tea.

DOLLY. When I said milky I didn't mean a whole udder full. I think you're doing this on purpose, Jude.

JUDE takes the cup to the sink and pours away the tea.

I wonder if there might be a biscuit at the back of the cupboard?

JUDE (*looking in the cupboard*). What sort of biscuit?

DOLLY. Something like a chocolate chip.

JUDE. No. Wait a minute, yes.

DOLLY. Esther was always fond of a chocolate-chip biscuit, nothing will alter that.

JUDE (*he puts the biscuits on the table and pours milk into DOLLY's cup*). Say when.

DOLLY. When. Once upon a time, she used to bake them and they were delicious.

ESTHER. Would you rather have a sandwich?

DOLLY. Thank you, darling Esther.

ESTHER. Ham and mustard because Dad loved the mustard we bought in the Dordogne, on those holidays in the farmhouse in Périgueux. I'll do some with and some without as Dad always used to.

She starts to make a sandwich with an uncut loaf from the bread bin and things from the fridge.

DOLLY (*she points*). The light bulb has gone. If you give me another one, I'll put it in for you.

JUDE finds a light bulb in a cupboard.

I keep on wondering if these darts are anything to do with you, Jude. It's as if Lucifer has been here, the devil himself.

DOLLY stands on a chair. JUDE holds it to keep it still, and then he shakes it. DOLLY wobbles and lets out a small shriek.

There's a little bit of wickedness in you. Give me time and I'm going to find out about it. (*She puts in the new bulb.*) I'm nervous enough of London as it is. I don't know why anyone would live here through choice.

The light goes on. JUDE helps DOLLY to get off the chair.

What else needs doing?

ESTHER. Nothing. Leave it now.

DOLLY. There must be something to do, there always is.
(*She looks about.*) It's somehow different in here. It used to
be a cold room and now it's lived in. I fancy it might be your
influence, Jude. Have you still got the kitchen upstairs?

ESTHER. Yes.

DOLLY. There was always plenty of room for a big family.

ESTHER. I've been used to paying a peppercorn rent, but it's
going up and up and up and up. This is the plate with
mustard.

DOLLY. Thank you, darling.

There are two plates of sandwiches on the table.

(*Pulling out a chair to sit on.*) Aren't you hungry, Jude?

JUDE. No.

DOLLY. Nibble. You're allowed to nibble.

ESTHER (*sitting*). Have you remembered we're going to
Dungeness on Wednesday?

JUDE. Yes, it's why I came back.

ESTHER. I think we'll still go. (*She turns to her sister.*) Quite
a few years ago I bought a cottage on Dungeness near the
power station.

DOLLY. I could be knocked over with a feather.

ESTHER. I can't remember if I've talked about the cottage or
not.

DOLLY. I have a good memory, I'm like an elephant.

ESTHER. It's a refuge.

DOLLY. A secret.

ESTHER. A quiet place.

DOLLY. No one knows about it.

ESTHER. A bolthole to get away to where I'm not disturbed.

DOLLY. On Wednesday. The day after tomorrow.

ESTHER. Yes.

DOLLY. But what about me?

ESTHER. There is room for you.

DOLLY. I want to be welcome.

ESTHER. There's two bedrooms, so we would have to share a bed.

JUDE. I can sleep on the sofa with some pillows and a duvet.

DOLLY (*she looks at her sister*). He doesn't behave like a lodger. When I see him behave like a lodger, I'll believe he is one.

ESTHER (*she gets up to put the biscuits in the cupboard*). I'm presuming you didn't want a biscuit.

DOLLY. Thank you, darling, a sandwich is plenty.

They are still. DOLLY *takes a sandwich.*

I would like to see your cottage. All this is so new to me. I know I upset you. I don't mean to. I don't do it on purpose. It's because I'm clumsy. I'm clumsy emotionally.

ESTHER. Sometimes silence is best, Dolly.

DOLLY. I'll put a handkerchief in my mouth from now on.

ESTHER. I don't always wish to share my world in the way you do.

DOLLY. I promise.

ESTHER. I'm private, and there's nothing wrong in being private.

DOLLY. I'm being told off.

ESTHER. You're not.

DOLLY. We're full of the most ridiculous misunderstandings.

ESTHER. Jude is a friend. That's all he is.

DOLLY. I see that now.

ESTHER. I do hope so.

DOLLY. I keep on getting the most terrible déjà vu. I've had it from the minute I arrived.

ESTHER. What. What about?

DOLLY. All this has happened before. I know it's what you're thinking, but I haven't come here because of Mummy.

ESTHER. Yes, I was thinking that.

DOLLY. I've come all this way from Harrogate because I've left Derek. My marriage is a sham.

ESTHER (*she refreshes* DOLLY*'s tea*). Men can be complete and utter beasts, Dolly.

DOLLY. After forty-nine years my marriage is finished. He's a philanderer. You will know all the words because you're clever.

ESTHER. The man is a shit and was never any different.

DOLLY. He's had affair after affair after affair, I found out yesterday. He even had an affair the week we were married, what a cunt he is. It's the first time I've ever used that reprehensible word, and I hate him for it. It's not a word we use in Harrogate, Jude, but it's been on the tip of my tongue and I'm glad to get it out.

ESTHER. Would you like a glass of wine?

DOLLY. A glass of wine would be lovely.

JUDE *goes to the fridge for a bottle*.

Don't you use the kitchen upstairs any longer?

ESTHER. It's somehow easier to live in here.

DOLLY. I know I don't go deep emotionally sometimes, but I'm still hurt. It's all been secrets and lies. I wonder if I don't go emotionally deep sometimes because somewhere in me I've known about him all along, I've just not acknowledged it until these moments now.

ESTHER *takes three glasses from a cupboard and puts them on the table*.

I haven't loved him for a long time. I've loved the
comfortable life he gave me.

JUDE *pours the wine*.

Derek was a builder, Jude. You would have enjoyed the big
house and the garden and the bank account.

ESTHER. Cheers.

DOLLY. He tried to appreciate a glass of wine, but Derek was
brought up on beer. I wasn't adventurous sexually in the
bedroom, or anywhere else. Now I realise he's been getting
his excitement elsewhere. Perhaps I'm glad. Jude's a man of
the world, I can speak my mind.

They drink.

I'm too close to seventy for comfort and I don't know a
thing. What is being in love?

ESTHER (*she drinks*). Isn't it wanting the best for someone
else?

DOLLY. Have you been in love?

ESTHER. I've wanted the best for another person.

DOLLY. You've never married. I've always wondered why
that is.

ESTHER (*she drinks*). My life didn't go that way.

DOLLY. I hope you've been happy.

ESTHER. It didn't take me in that direction.

DOLLY. I would blame myself if you were lonely.

ESTHER. If you write you must like your own company, it's as
simple as that.

DOLLY. You didn't start writing until you were forty and more.

ESTHER (*she drinks*). I can't write if someone else is close by.
(*She tops up her glass*.) Writing isn't a way to be perfectly
happy, but to be in love isn't perfect either.

DOLLY. Why didn't you like Derek?

ESTHER. I didn't know him, Dolly. We were polite, and that isn't enough to know someone.

DOLLY. Sometimes he talked about you fondly as if you did.

ESTHER (*she drinks*). I saw him once in a blue moon.

DOLLY. He found you cryptic and mysterious, a sort of crossword clue.

ESTHER. That was clever of him.

DOLLY. He said you did clandestine things. I realise now he was talking about himself as much as you. Did you know he wasn't faithful to me, Esther darling?

ESTHER. No, I didn't.

DOLLY. You're intelligent.

ESTHER. You exaggerate my intelligence and always have.

DOLLY (*she gets up*). My legs are still stiff from the car. He was a terrible womaniser. I think he might have been addicted to casual sex. Did you know?

ESTHER. How would I know such a thing, Dolly?

DOLLY. You knew him as well as me.

ESTHER. Did I? Don't be so silly. I didn't know him as well as you.

DOLLY. Derek told me something, Esther darling, and I want you to tell me it isn't true and it's a lie.

ESTHER. What?

DOLLY. He said the day before our wedding day, you and him had sex together beside the cherry tree in the garden at home.

ESTHER *sips her wine*.

And I can see by your reaction that it's all true. You're not clever at this second.

ESTHER. It's not true, Dolly.

DOLLY. You're a liar. I'm going to have the tree chopped down.

ESTHER. I would not do that to anyone, let alone you.

DOLLY. Yes, you would.

ESTHER. I didn't care for Derek.

DOLLY. I know, and that's why I'm completely baffled about the whole thing. I'm going to cut the cherry tree down, and then we'll sell Mum's house.

A silence.

ESTHER. I've been feeling guilty about it all my life.

DOLLY. So, it's true. You had sex with my husband before I did.

ESTHER. Yes.

  DOLLY *slaps* ESTHER. *She grabs* ESTHER*'s hair.*
  ESTHER *grabs* DOLLY*'s hair.* JUDE *throws his glass of wine over them. A silence. He refills his glass.* ESTHER *goes to the sink to sprinkle water on her face.*

  I am truly sorry.

DOLLY. It's not big enough, I need a bigger sorry than that.

ESTHER. All my adult life I've been frightened of this day.

DOLLY. I want to know why, Esther darling?

ESTHER. I was young, and I was flirty.

DOLLY. You were selfish and took whatever you wanted.

ESTHER. He approached me, I didn't go to him.

DOLLY. Liar. I don't want any more of your rubbish. It was both of you. (*She drinks.*) Your own wine doesn't get you drunk, isn't that what they say if you own a vineyard. I bought some shares in one in France for a little hobby. It doesn't work with me. My husband's hobby was the opposite sex from before we were married. Why did he ask me to marry him? I must have had something he wanted.

ESTHER. You were beautiful, you turned heads.

DOLLY. I know I was attractive.

ESTHER. I didn't turn heads.

DOLLY. You were beautiful to me.

ESTHER. You caught the eye of everyone.

DOLLY. Did I? Are you sure? Not everyone.

ESTHER. I was envious of the attention.

DOLLY (*she drinks*). I haven't had sex in a garden. It was a February day, there was a thick frost. We were married in a leap year, Jude, on the extra day. I thought it would make the marriage extra-special forever.

ESTHER. I can't turn back the clock.

DOLLY. You can have him, keep him, he's yours, the abysmal man.

ESTHER. I wish I did have some magic to fly back in time.

DOLLY. I don't ever want to catch a sight of him.

ESTHER. I wish I could begin again and do life differently.

DOLLY (*she takes keys from her coat and throws them*). Here's the keys, take them, have everything, take the lot, go to him, drive up there now. I can tell it's what you want.

ESTHER. Life isn't something we can undo, like a piece of knitting.

DOLLY. I'm not bothered, I don't care about anything any longer. I just don't give a jot for you. You had everything. In one single moment you've ruined my entire life.

JUDE *is moving his finger around the top of his glass making a high-pitched note.* DOLLY *throws her glass of wine over* ESTHER. JUDE *throws his glass of wine over* DOLLY. *A silence.*

I think you're a little bit of a gangster, young man, student, lodger, whoever you are. Lover, wouldn't surprise me.

JUDE. At the moment I'm not in love. I don't know if love will come to me, but I hope so. You feel rejected. My mother once put my soiled underpants in my mouth. She used to slap me and bite me. Esther is generous and gives me a room when I want it and has done for fifteen years since I was twelve. (*He stammers.*) Shall I, shall I, shall I refresh your glass?

(*He pours wine*.) She'd she'd she'd she'd wrap me in wine-soaked bedclothes. Your sister sister has never done that.

ESTHER *sprinkles water on her face.* JUDE *takes the clothes from the washing machine and folds them neatly.* DOLLY *goes to the sink and sprinkles water on her face.* ESTHER *takes an ironing board from the wardrobe and finds an iron. She plugs it in.* DOLLY *takes a shirt and some clothes from* JUDE*'s pile. She starts to iron.* JUDE *picks up the keys, goes out and up the steps to park the car.*

DOLLY. He has a stammer.

ESTHER. He has a stammer only sometimes, Dolly.

DOLLY. He sounded like Daddy when he stammered. Daddy was only sometimes.

ESTHER. You probably won't hear it again. (*She picks up the rest of the clothes and puts them on the end of the ironing board.*) When he was twelve, he stammered so badly I struggled to understand him. Jude is full of foibles.

DOLLY. The same as Daddy was full of foibles.

ESTHER. Yes, why not.

DOLLY (*she has some pants*). What about these articles?

ESTHER (*she puts the ironed shirt on the table*). No, leave those.

DOLLY. We have a home-help for all this. I'd love to iron a boy's clothes, vests, pants shirts, muddy football shorts, but it didn't happen. We weren't blessed with little feet. If I let myself be it, I could be envious.

ESTHER. What of and why?

DOLLY. Your independent life in London. I don't really have friends, I have people I talk to. How did you meet?

ESTHER. How did I meet who, Dolly?

DOLLY. How did you meet Jude?

ESTHER. He followed me home, knocked on the door and asked for a biscuit, except he didn't say it, he wrote it in a notebook with biscuit spelt with a k. He came with a kitten in his arms that became a cat. Jeremy, but Jeremy had kittens on his bed, lost her tail in a fight, and died only a few weeks ago.

DOLLY. It's a fairy story.

ESTHER. I didn't find him, he found me, like cats do.

DOLLY. It could only happen in London.

ESTHER. Jude decides, he makes up his own mind and always has. I'm not an influence. Let me do that.

DOLLY. I can run the hoover over if you like.

ESTHER (*taking over the ironing*). Does it need it?

DOLLY. A floor could always do with a hoover run over it, but not really.

ESTHER. As a rule, Jude does his own ironing. It was part of his pocket money, when he was small.

DOLLY. I'm envious of you being a mother.

ESTHER. I'm not a mother.

DOLLY. A sort of mother.

ESTHER. He had a mother. He moved to and fro between the two places.

DOLLY. You didn't like cats.

ESTHER. I managed to like Jeremy.

DOLLY. What happened to the kittens?

ESTHER. We found homes for them eventually. Jeremy was Jude's cat. She was his responsibility.

DOLLY. Who buys his clothes?

ESTHER. He does. Who else would buy his clothes, Dolly?

DOLLY. I was meaning when he was twelve.

ESTHER. When he was twelve, I gave him an allowance. It was up to him if he bought sweets with it. I think he bought crisps.

DOLLY (*she unplugs the vacuum cleaner*). I used to put my dolls in the bath.

ESTHER. I expect you still do.

DOLLY. And make them breakfast before school. They have
    made for a lonely life.

ESTHER. You should throw them away.

DOLLY. I can't. I'd like to, but I can't.

ESTHER. I know, Dolly, and I know how much you wanted a
    home with children in it.

DOLLY. Does the vacuum cleaner still go in here?

ESTHER. Yes, in there.

DOLLY (*she puts the vacuum cleaner in the wardrobe*). Did
    you put Jude in the bath?

ESTHER. He was twelve, he would not have thanked me if I'd
    put him in the bath. He could wash himself. Forget about it,
    Dolly. A mother sees her child naked. I've not once seen Jude
    in his birthday suit. I've made every effort not to be his mother.

    DOLLY *closes the wardrobe door, which falls off.*

    Don't worry about it, it does that. Jude will fix it, which is
    why it keeps falling off.

DOLLY. Has he passed the driving test?

ESTHER. I don't know, I don't think he has.

DOLLY. Are you serious?

ESTHER. He drives me about, we don't hit much.

DOLLY. My car is full of dents, I don't suppose another crash
    will make much difference.

ESTHER. I'm joking.

    The sound of a piano being played drifts into the room.

DOLLY. Who's playing the piano?

ESTHER. It's Buster, the boy at the top, his mother is an
    actress, he's eighteen and he can't sleep, so already he is
    troubled. We're all mixed up, Dolly. Somehow everything is
    in the wrong place, at odds with itself, we're all disjointed.
    I'm sorry about everything that's happened this evening.

    DOLLY *tries to put the door on the wardrobe.*

Scene Two

A great electricity pylon rises out of the shingle that covers Dungeness. Some way up is barbed wire to stop anybody foolish enough climbing further. For all we know the top of the pylon might touch the clouds.

ESTHER *and* DOLLY *are apart.* ESTHER *walks and takes in the morning sun, already hot.* DOLLY *looks at the pylon and is made small by its size.*

DOLLY. So, this is Dungeness.

ESTHER. Yes, it's the only desert in Europe.

DOLLY (*she looks at a pile of things, a bag, some clothes, a towel on the shingle*). Are these Jude's things? If I'm not careful, this will become a holiday. (*She looks out.*) The English Channel. A strip of water that keeps us all safe. (*She turns.*) The famous nuclear power station that even I've heard of from when we were young girls. Where does the electricity go?

ESTHER. I like to think the wires go all the way to Little Venice in one unbroken line.

DOLLY. How long have you been coming here?

ESTHER. It must be thirty years since I bought the cottage, but I don't count time, my arithmetic isn't good enough.

DOLLY. It's a long-held secret.

ESTHER. Shy people do sometimes keep secrets.

DOLLY. I'll have to think about that one.

ESTHER (*walking somewhere*). The walks here are very good, the thinking time is like the air, very clear, and it's away from the noise of London streets.

DOLLY. I can smell the traffic in London. Will you ever come back home?

ESTHER. My home hasn't been in Yorkshire for so long I can't remember how long.

DOLLY. Home is always where we're born.

ESTHER (*walking*). It isn't in my case.

DOLLY. If only you belonged somewhere, you wouldn't be so restless.

ESTHER. Nothing has ever escaped your beady mind, or stopped you having an opinion. I got into the grammar school and you didn't...

DOLLY. I was educationally challenged...

ESTHER. It should have been the other way about...

DOLLY. Should it?

ESTHER. The truth is, you were the brainy one, cleverer than me by a long way.

DOLLY. I was always pleased for you. I knew, even at school, that I would have to marry the right person to have a good life, and that it wasn't about being in love it was about money.

They both walk somewhere.

ESTHER. I've written the novels here every summer. Now and again in the winter months if I couldn't finish them, whenever I had time away from college teaching. Every summer except this summer now. The last book went in the rubbish bin, all one hundred and eighty-eight pages of it. My editor asked for changes and I don't do changes. If I seem restless it's because I'm used to writing.

DOLLY. I write shopping lists, which are challenging enough.

ESTHER. Have you read the books?

DOLLY. Once upon a time I did try to read them.

ESTHER. I'll give them to you next birthday if you like.

DOLLY. You didn't seem bothered either way. I was always told everything in them was cleverer than me.

ESTHER. The books are full of lies, Dolly.

DOLLY. That's another one I'll have to think about. Derek read every book.

ESTHER. Did he?

DOLLY. Have you made a lot of money?

ESTHER. I've made some money. What did Derek think?

DOLLY. He told me I wouldn't comprehend them, I remember the word, and I accepted that, because we do believe what our husbands tell us in Harrogate. (*She looks at the sea.*) Does the little dot out there belong to Jude? Is that him in the sea swimming?

ESTHER. Yes, it is.

DOLLY. He's not who you think he is.

ESTHER. Do you remember when we were children I stuck a Biro in your hand?

DOLLY. Yes, and I remember it hurt like a bee sting.

ESTHER. If I had a Biro now I'd do the same thing.

DOLLY. Three and three does not make six. With Jude everything makes seven.

ESTHER (*she walks*). You carry your prejudice with you for the same reasons that a snail carries a shell.

DOLLY. He's a strong swimmer. What am I prejudiced about?

ESTHER. Your Yorkshire suspicions.

DOLLY (*she looks at the sea*). A boat. A lot of ships all going somewhere in the world. I wasn't suggesting he loves you for your money…

ESTHER. You were suggesting something…

DOLLY. I was thinking of you…

ESTHER. Please don't think of me…

DOLLY. I can if I want to…

ESTHER. I'm tired of it.

A foghorn sounds from a ship.

DOLLY. I'm jealous, Esther, and perhaps a little bit more than that. I'd be happy to love a bad man, if only he loved me. I'm so alone, Esther darling. I haven't children. Life didn't smile on me in that way. You are the only family I have in the world. In the last few days all my friends have become completely meaningless, and I don't know why, but I'm less worried when I'm with you.

ESTHER. I'm sorry I stuck the Biro in your hand…

DOLLY. Do you remember…

ESTHER. It's something I've never forgotten…

DOLLY (*she touches the back of her hand*). I've still got the blue mark it left on my skin. (*She walks and picks up a shell.*) Why didn't you get married? Didn't you fall in love until Jude…

ESTHER. I am not in love with Jude…

DOLLY. I'm sorry…

ESTHER. If you are not very careful, Dolly, I'll go off and come back with a Biro…

DOLLY. How old were we…

ESTHER. When…

DOLLY. The Biro incident…

ESTHER. We would have been twelve or thirteen…

DOLLY. The silly age. I had a friend who told me she'd never been in love. At the time I thought, what a sad life, however much love hurts. It's just occurred to me that perhaps you loved Derek. I made up the friend. I wonder if I might be right.

ESTHER. I'd be more likely to love the Pope, or Hitler. Derek doesn't have a single opinion I care about. And he's an ugly man, who wears a hat. Never trust a man who wears a hat indoors.

DOLLY. When the divorce goes through I'll get half his money, perhaps I did the clever thing after all. He's at least a millionaire. (*She picks up a shell.*) I don't think of you as shy.

ESTHER. It's quite clear we don't know each other, like too many other families.

DOLLY. Have you secrets hidden away?

ESTHER. Have I secrets of what hidden where?

DOLLY. I want to know you.

ESTHER (*she walks*). Shall I tell you a secret a day from now on, think of it as like a pill.

DOLLY. Yes, please, I would like that.

ESTHER. I worry about you...

DOLLY. Is a secret coming?

ESTHER. I worry about your need for reassurance every minute, like when we were schoolgirls. (*She walks.*) I can't put the fun back into your life, only you can do that.

ESTHER *picks up a shell.*

DOLLY. I'm still waiting for a secret.

DOLLY *picks up a shell.*

A friend told me that shells travel the oceans, they can have come from anywhere in the world.

ESTHER. Is this another friend who lives in your imagination?

DOLLY. No, she's real. I do believe the things people tell me.

They look at one another.

ESTHER. The books are lies because I've written about being in love all the time, page after page, but, like some of your friends, it's all made up and in my head, it's not true, I've an imagination. (*She picks up another shell.*) I wrote that we don't find love, but that love finds us. It didn't want to be found by me.

DOLLY. Are you angry?

ESTHER. Why did you ask that...

DOLLY. I don't know why I asked...

ESTHER. Perhaps in life I am angry. (*She picks up a third shell.*) I wrote a novel about sex, and strangely it was quite good. What I really know about sex could be put on the back of a stamp.

A foghorn sounds from a boat.

DOLLY (*she looks at the sea*). Jude will be getting cold. You should call him in.

ESTHER. He's not a child. If I had a child, I wouldn't call him in…

DOLLY. He's as slippery as an eel…

ESTHER. He's only slippery in your slightly odd imagination…

DOLLY. What does he do and how does he live…

ESTHER. Why don't you ask him…

DOLLY. I'm asking you, Esther.

ESTHER. I think he sells cannabis and cocaine to the people who live on the boats along the canal. He grows cannabis plants.

DOLLY. My hair should go up on end, but I'm not altogether surprised.

ESTHER *looks at the shells she has picked up. She puts them down on the shingle, one by one, in different places.*

ESTHER. I worry about him. I worry more about him at least as much now as I did when he was a boy. He listened to me then, and I could bribe him with a present.

DOLLY. I won't be critical, I wouldn't dare. He's a drug-dealer…

ESTHER. Don't you have them in Harrogate…

DOLLY. I'm told the town is awash with drugs. When did he start dealing in drugs?

ESTHER. He came to me when he was twelve…

DOLLY. Was he doing it then?

ESTHER. I think he was, but it's a guess, and it's different now…

DOLLY. That is young…

ESTHER. It's too young…

DOLLY. It's very young. It's such a shame. You should have put
    your foot down and said a motherly no no no...

ESTHER. I have sleepless nights, like a parent has sleepless
    nights, but he's a friend, Dolly, he's not my child. If I'd been
    too critical, he would have run off to someone else, and been
    in more danger.

DOLLY. Did he come here to Dungeness when he was twelve?

ESTHER. Yes, he did. He would go swimming every morning
    and leave me to work, like clockwork, that was the routine.
    He made the garden around the house, which I keep meaning
    to tidy up. The garden is his. It's a remarkable achievement
    because it's a desert.

DOLLY (*she turns the shell over in her fingers*). I've not been
    lucky enough to have a child like Jude come into my life.

ESTHER. That shell is from Madagascar.

DOLLY. How can you tell?

ESTHER. It's the colours of the flag.

DOLLY. Here he is.

    JUDE *comes on, in a pair of shorts, from the sea.*

JUDE. Why don't you come in the sea? It's the best sort of
    breakfast.

DOLLY. I can't swim. The nearest I ever got to deep water was
    in the bath.

JUDE (*he picks up his towel*). How ridiculous. You must learn
    immediately.

DOLLY. As a child, we didn't have seaside holidays where
    I might have taken the plunge. As an adult, we went to
    Cape Town and Rio de Janeiro and did cities, ticked them
    off so we could show off. I'd like to buy some cannabis from
    you, Jude.

ESTHER. Dolly, a secret isn't a secret unless you keep it...

DOLLY. I'm sure Jude doesn't mind another customer.

ESTHER. You are wrong a hundred times.

JUDE. What's a hundred times a hundred times a hundred again?

DOLLY. I'm sorry.

JUDE. The number is how much you're wrong. (*He looks at* ESTHER.) A trust has been broken, this and that has been said about me, and it's private.

ESTHER. It's a mistake, Jude. When you have made a mistake, life has not come to an end, the world has gone on as far as I know.

JUDE (*he covers his face with the towel*). You're not my life, Esther. What I am is nothing to do with you. You should be sorry, Dolly. (*He dries his hair.*) Sorry is an easy word. I was told sorry repeatedly. (*He dries his hair.*) No one is hurt. (*He dries his hair.*) My mother used to say sorry.

DOLLY. Where is your mother, Jude?

JUDE. She's nowhere, she's dead as a doorknob, scattered to the wind. She died when I was sixteen and two months.

DOLLY. Did you love her?

JUDE. I don't know. How can you love someone who lashes out and is vicious?

DOLLY. It is possible to love those people. I know because Derek hit me once or twice, not much, but once or twice is enough.

JUDE. It wasn't my mother's fault.

DOLLY. It was her fault, just as it was Derek's fault when he hit me. He thumped me so hard in Kuala Lumpur I needed stitches inside my mouth.

JUDE. It must have hurt.

DOLLY. It did hurt.

JUDE. It still hurts. (*He picks up his things.*) Will you be here for a minute or two? I'll go and get changed over there. I don't want any of us to be embarrassed.

ESTHER. We'll wait here for you, take as long as you need to. Breakfast won't spoil for a few minutes. It's a lovely morning.

JUDE (*he hangs his bag on the pylon and looks at* DOLLY).
I don't sell cannabis plants, I give them away for presents in kind. One plant is two shirts or a side of beef, two plants a pair of trousers.

DOLLY. I think I can afford three.

JUDE. Three is a foreign, European holiday.

DOLLY. If it's not a city, it will be my pleasure.

JUDE *goes off to get changed.*

You're Tweedledee and Tweedledum, two peas in a pod.
Why are you both so quiet, and private? I'm noisy, it can't be helped, but sometimes noise is good. There's a need for shallow people in the world. We can't all be complicated.

ESTHER. When did you go to Kuala Lumpur?

DOLLY. It's quite a few years ago. Being hit by your husband is a very sad thing to admit to, but I'm pleased I did.

ESTHER. I didn't realise you had such an unhappy marriage, goodness it must have nagged away.

DOLLY (*she walks*). Jude is the first person I've told about the violence. He made me spill the beans and I don't really know why. I can see his willy.

ESTHER. Where?

They both look.

JUDE (*off*). Stop looking.

ESTHER. What did he say?

DOLLY. He told us to stop looking.

ESTHER. We'd better do as we're told.

JUDE (*off*). Tell Esther I've written a play.

ESTHER. What did he say?

DOLLY. He says to tell you he's written a play.

ESTHER. What?

DOLLY (*calling*). She says what.

JUDE (*off*). I've been wanting to tell her for weeks.

DOLLY. He's been wanting to tell you for weeks.

JUDE (*off*). I've been waiting to find the right moment.

DOLLY. He's been waiting to find the right moment to tell you.

JUDE (*off*). There's a copy in my bag.

DOLLY. He says there's a copy of the play in his bag.

> ESTHER *searches in* JUDE's *bag and finds a book. She looks at it carefully, and then turns the pages.*

> Did you not know?

ESTHER (*she shakes her head*). No, I'd not an inkling. (S*he looks in the book.*) It was on at the Royal Court. It's a famous London theatre. It's not a theatre in a room in a pub on the corner of the street, or in a tent.

DOLLY. Why didn't he tell you?

JUDE (*off*). I didn't tell her because I was embarrassed.

ESTHER (*calling*). Why were you embarrassed?

JUDE (*off*). I thought it was no good.

DOLLY. He says he thought it was no good.

ESTHER. Why?

DOLLY (*calling*). She wants to know why? (*She looks at her sister.*) I can tell you why. He's got it into his head that he is no good. It travels through life, it happens when people hit us.

JUDE (*off*). Tell her I know I'm useless.

DOLLY. He says he's useless.

JUDE (*off*). I thought I'd be found out and the world would tumble down like in an earthquake.

ESTHER. Tell him he's not useless.

DOLLY. I won't, I'm not a servant.

ESTHER. Ask him what the play is about.

JUDE (*he comes on. He is dressed*). It's about a young dealer who goes to Norway to find the grandfather he's never met and doesn't know, but instead he meets a girl and falls in love which changes everything.

ESTHER. Is it about your grandfather in Norway?

JUDE. The character is Gabriel Twelvetrees and was a pop singer in the 1960s. He's an old pothead who lives in a cottage offstage. We don't see him.

ESTHER. Your grandfather, or a man who might possibly be him.

JUDE. Yes. The theatre said the writing was like a muddy canal. I've not been to Norway. The lies came easily, and everyone wanted to believe them.

ESTHER. Is the play still on?

JUDE. No, it's ended.

ESTHER. When did it finish?

JUDE. The charade came to an end on Saturday with a party. I want to be a writer, but unluckily for me I'm not strong enough, or confident.

ESTHER. Why didn't you tell me about the play?

JUDE (*shrugs*). I don't know.

ESTHER. Didn't you want me to see it?

JUDE (*shrugs*). I don't know. I did want you to see the play, but it's too late. I couldn't find the courage to tell you, I was only able to summon up the courage this minute.

ESTHER (*she looks at the play*). Now I know where you've been these last few weeks, the disappearing trick.

JUDE. I've been busier than ever.

ESTHER. What about your friends, what about Harry?

JUDE. Harry's the only one. He came to the opening night and a few other times.

ESTHER. Tell him it's all too much for one day.

DOLLY. He's got ears in his head and I know they work.

JUDE. Are you angry with me, Esther?

ESTHER. I keep looking for a cigarette, but I don't smoke any longer. No.

JUDE. Are you upset?

ESTHER. No. Why would I be?

JUDE. I don't want you to be those things, especially upset.

ESTHER. I was worrying something was seriously wrong, and the police were going to knock on the door in the early hours of the morning looking for you. It's pointless to tell me I shouldn't be anxious.

JUDE. You shouldn't be anxious.

ESTHER. I know, but to tell me is pointless, Jude.

JUDE. You are angry, I don't blame you.

ESTHER. I'm telling you that I care about you.

JUDE. Yes, I'm a selfish good-for-nothing who doesn't deserve it.

ESTHER (*she looks at the book*). We need to know about our families, so you should go to Norway, talk to your grandfather, if you can find him and he'll see you.

JUDE. It goes around my head at night when I can't sleep, I want to do something special with the money from the play.

ESTHER. Inventing a story won't make you happy, it can make the loneliness worse, the isolation.

The morning is pierced by the sound of a herring gull on top of the pylon.

Don't forget the towel over there.

JUDE. No. It's an old one that's gone like cardboard.

JUDE goes off.

DOLLY. Why have so many boats been left to rot all over the place? It's a boat cemetery. And the big pieces of rusting metal sticking up, there must be a reason for them. It's crazy. It's like God got angry and chucked some old boats at the earth.

ESTHER. Think of it as art, Dungeness is an exhibition on a grand scale, and I like it.

DOLLY. Jude is sitting on a boat. He has a handful of pebbles. It's so obvious you wanted a child...

ESTHER. Is it? Obvious to who?

DOLLY. You would have been a very good mother.

ESTHER. I'd have been a hopeless mother, Dolly, too full of myself.

DOLLY. We're both of us unhappy where children are concerned.

ESTHER. I'm not unhappy.

DOLLY. I think you are unhappy. I think you're really upset that Jude didn't tell you about his play.

ESTHER. I have a child.

DOLLY. Jude is beautiful in his own way, once you get to know him.

ESTHER. I'm not talking about Jude. I have a child. Somewhere I have a child. A boy. I have a boy of my own somewhere. A little boy. He's still tiny in my mind. He was three weeks old when I saw him last. A tiny baby boy.

A silence.

DOLLY. I don't believe you. If it's true, why didn't you tell me?

ESTHER. It was my business, Dolly, it wasn't your business.

There is the sound of the herring gull.

DOLLY. When was he born?

ESTHER. I was a student, I was far too young.

DOLLY. I must be a fool. All these long years it's been a secret. I did think there was something in our genes about children and why we didn't have them. (*She is looking.*) Jude is throwing pebbles like he does darts. Does he know?

ESTHER. He knows something of Oliver.

DOLLY. Oliver, it's a gorgeous name. I keep imagining he's mine.

ESTHER. I don't know how it's happened, but Jude is my closest friend.

DOLLY (*she walks somewhere and stops*). I'm finding this very hard to believe. I still don't believe you. Where is Oliver now?

ESTHER. I don't know.

DOLLY. How old is the little boy, you must know that.

ESTHER. He will be fifty next year.

DOLLY. I was seeing a toddler in his first pair of shoes. Would you lie to me, Esther?

ESTHER. Yes, but not about this.

DOLLY. How old were you when Oliver was born?

ESTHER. I've already said I was far too young.

DOLLY. How old is far too young?

ESTHER. Why does it matter how young I was?

DOLLY (*she walks somewhere*). Were you eighteen?

ESTHER (*she walks somewhere*). I wasn't eighteen.

DOLLY. Were you nineteen?

ESTHER. I wasn't nineteen.

DOLLY. Were you twenty?

A slight pause.

You were twenty, that is very young. Who was the little boy's father?

ESTHER. He was nobody, Dolly.

DOLLY. He was somebody, poor man.

ESTHER. He wasn't a poor man.

DOLLY. Did he know he had a child?

ESTHER. I didn't tell him.

DOLLY. Why not?

ESTHER. He didn't need to know. No one knew. It was my secret. I did what seemed to be the right thing at that time.

DOLLY. He would be a student at the college like you, I suspect.

ESTHER. No. (*She walks.*) I was so naive I didn't know I was pregnant for quite a few months. I still find it incredible considering Dad was a doctor. My head was full of the suffering of the world, the visionaries and thinkers. I didn't notice my own suffering. I pretended I wasn't pregnant until it became impossible to pretend any longer, and out he popped one morning, almost a surprise.

DOLLY. What did he look like?

ESTHER. He looked like a newly born child.

DOLLY. I was asking you if he was gorgeous?

ESTHER (*she walks*). If it happened today I'd know he was beautiful, but at the time I didn't look properly. I don't know how many times I have to say it, I wasn't a natural mother. I looked at babies and saw babies. I looked at Oliver and saw a baby.

JUDE *comes on with the wet towel.*

JUDE. What are you talking about?

ESTHER. Oliver. Dolly doesn't know, I've just been filling her in. We'll have breakfast at the pub. Why don't you go ahead and find us a table.

JUDE. I've got bacon and sausage and eggs and fried bread and mushrooms, I can put them on the stove and you can follow me back in a minute.

ESTHER. I'd rather go to the pub this morning, we should say hello.

JUDE. Have you shown her the photograph?

ESTHER. Don't be silly, it's in London.

DOLLY. Have you a photograph of Oliver?

ESTHER. I've one photograph.

DOLLY. I just can't imagine letting him go to someone who wasn't his mother. If we hold our child, he's ours.

ESTHER (*she looks at the play*). Can I keep this?

JUDE. It was in my bag waiting for you.

ESTHER. I'm sure I'll have something to say another time, but for now, thank you. A first book is incredibly special.

JUDE. I can't stop myself reading it.

ESTHER. Maybe a first book is as special as a first child, or maybe nothing can replace a child. I'm not a monster, Dolly, I did what I thought was best for Oliver and for me.

DOLLY. I would be weeping uncontrollably.

ESTHER. Perhaps I am, perhaps something inside me is weeping uncontrollably and has been for a long time, but my being distraught doesn't make the world happier, or living any more bearable.

DOLLY. I see things the simple way.

ESTHER. If I hear that one more time I shall scream like Violet Elizabeth Bott.

DOLLY. I married a simple man so that my life would be easy. I've always done the easiest thing, and it must stop.

ESTHER. This is not about you. You are not the one who is hurt.

DOLLY. I'm very sorry. What did you just say?

ESTHER. I said you're not the one who's hurt.

DOLLY. You've had a child and I'm not hurt?

DOLLY *walks*.

Something is nagging away, something is itching, I don't know what or why or how. I don't ever mean to be selfish. When friends have children, you can never be completely friends with them. I know I'm self-centred, it comes from being childless. It nags away that Derek is the father, that would completely kill me. You must have had sex a lot at that time. Did you?

ESTHER. No, I didn't.

DOLLY. I'm sorry for being so personal, Jude.

JUDE. You do think about yourself, Dolly.

DOLLY. Do I?

JUDE. Yes, all the time.

DOLLY. I can't stop it. (*She looks at her sister.*) Who was Oliver's father?

ESTHER. We quarrel, but I would never want to kill you.

DOLLY. Has she told you?

JUDE. No.

DOLLY. What a fibber you are, Jude.

JUDE. I've not told a fib ever in my life.

ESTHER. Jude doesn't know, stop guessing.

DOLLY. He seems to know the whole story.

ESTHER. He doesn't know the whole story. I've not told him how much it hurts when I think about Oliver now. I've never quite grown up because I gave him away. I would love to be with him. I sometimes think as I go down the street has he just walked past me. Did I go by him and not see? If I'd been a second later, would we have bumped.

A slight pause.

I had sex with Derek gladly, and it was wrong of me. And he is Oliver's father, Dolly.

JUDE. Both of you count to ten.

A slight pause.

ESTHER. The knowledge has stayed quietly within me. You're the first person I've told, and to know.

A slight pause.

DOLLY. Even Jude?

ESTHER. Even Jude.

DOLLY. Even Derek?

ESTHER. Even Derek.

ESTHER faints.

JUDE (*he goes to help*). You've just gone over.

ESTHER (*she is already picking herself up*). Yes, I fell over. I did a little topple for some reason.

The herring gull calls and flies off.

JUDE. Are you better now?

ESTHER. Yes, I'm very good. We should go and get breakfast, before the pub fills up.

DOLLY. Why didn't you tell me a long time ago?

ESTHER. The truth only works, Dolly, if everybody tells it, and nobody does. I'm not cruel. Perhaps we're both cruel when neither of us means to be.

A slight pause.

DOLLY. Whereabouts is the pub?

ESTHER. It's not far. It's about a fifteen-minute walk.

A foghorn sounds from a ship.

DOLLY. I can't get over how strange Dungeness is. For a desert it's full of mischief. I can see why you're at home here. Are you glad you've told me, is it a weight off your mind?

ESTHER (*she walks*). It's too soon to know. Ask me again in a day or two. (*She stops walking.*) I thought everything would be so much easier if I let him go, for him, but it was wrong for me. He didn't go. I thought over time I'd forget about him, but of course I didn't, I couldn't. I gave part of me away. Something in me is missing and only one person can put it back. The emptiness doesn't get any better. Oliver ruined my life. Or my life went a different way, how can a child ruin anyone's life. I wish I'd not looked at him, not seen his face. It's strange I kept a photograph, but it's the most precious thing. Oliver still turns me over and mixes me up. It's not a memory, it's real. It makes me feel wrong to have been born.

A slight pause.

DOLLY. Which way is the pub?

ESTHER. It's along the beach that way.

JUDE. You both go, and I'll catch you up.

A silence.

ESTHER. I think I must ask you to forgive me.

A slight pause.

DOLLY. I'm not sure I can.

ESTHER. It's the clever thing to do.

DOLLY. Yes, I can see that. (*She walks somewhere.*) As a child, Jude, we had a collection box for Dr Barnardo's that I put some of my pocket money in every week. One Saturday instead of putting it in, I broke it and took the money out. You're the first person I've ever told.

JUDE. It's not too much to worry about.

DOLLY. I still think about it.

JUDE. You're lucky.

DOLLY. All this is too new. I don't like to be challenged. I should go off and find a cave to live in. I couldn't live with myself, Esther, if I'd been as horrible as this, as terrible as you…

JUDE. Abalone balderdash catastrophe dense electricity final…

DOLLY. What are you doing?

JUDE. I have to go through the alphabet, every time you stop me I'll only have to start again. Afresh biochemistry catapult denounce earthling family grounded harangue institution justice karma longevity man nonsense orange peel quarantine robust symmetry terrace underling vengeance wilful X-ray yellow zodiac.

A slight pause.

DOLLY. If you didn't want Oliver, I would have cared for him and brought him up. Why wasn't I asked? Why didn't you turn to me? I would have loved him.

ESTHER. I expected to be Auntie Esther, giving birthday presents. I thought there'd be lots of little feet.

DOLLY. Did you think I'd be a terrible mother?

ESTHER. I thought you'd be a loving mother.

DOLLY. I know who I am, and I know I'm damaged. The one thing I wanted more than anything I couldn't have. Derek wouldn't countenance us adopting a boy. When people don't have children there's always a story. I'll go along to the pub in a minute. I need to be with my own thoughts, which is unusual for me. I'd like to pay for you to go to Norway to meet your grandfather, but I don't want the plants.

JUDE. Thank you.

DOLLY. Tell Esther I was meaning to be sympathetic.

ESTHER. It was you who stole the money out of the money box?

DOLLY. Yes.

ESTHER. I was punished for that.

DOLLY. It could only be one of us two. You were troublemaker-in-chief.

ESTHER. If you walk back along the beach the way we came and a minute or two further you'll come to the pub on your left.

DOLLY *goes off to the pub*. ESTHER *puts her hands on her knees*.

JUDE. How are you?

ESTHER. Don't ask me. She's dreadful. (*She walks*.) She takes me back to when we were twelve and I know why I wanted to leave, the claustrophobia. She puts me in jail with even the small things she says. If I had something to hand, like a plate or a cup, or better still expensive porcelain, I'd smash it. I need a dollop of angry pleasure to help me face the rest of the day.

JUDE. You mean you've been happier?

ESTHER. It's not even ten o'clock.

JUDE (*he picks up a bottle*). Will this do?

ESTHER. What for?

JUDE. Something to smash.

ESTHER (*taking the bottle*). Thank you. There's a message inside.

JUDE. Where?

ESTHER. There. There's a piece of paper. It's a bottle with a message. (*She holds the bottle up to the light and turns it over in her fingers.*) It looks as if it might be in French, but water has smudged the ink.

JUDE. Give it to me.

ESTHER. Give it to me please.

JUDE (*he tries to open it*). It's stuck and rusted. I could smash the top?

ESTHER. People come along in their bare feet.

JUDE (*he holds the bottle up to the light*). It's about now I wish I'd gone to school and paid attention and was virtuous and learnt French.

ESTHER (*she takes the bottle*). Luckily for both of us, I did go to school. It looks like Amandine Caron, maybe, aged ten, something something, Glace Bay, Nova Scotia.

JUDE. Where's Nova Scotia?

ESTHER (*she gives him the bottle*). It's in Canada.

JUDE. I got geography blind for a moment.

ESTHER. You'd be educationally less blind if you'd gone to school once or twice and not bunked off for months on end.

JUDE. I'm brilliant at words. In life you only need to be good at one thing.

ESTHER (*she looks at the book*). Yes. I've always known you were good with words.

JUDE. We must reply immediately.

ESTHER. I'm sure you will, but first you'll have to buckle down and learn some French words.

JUDE (*he holds the bottle up to the light*). I can drive Dolly back to London if she's any more trouble. (*He picks up a plastic gun.*) I learnt a lot about you that I didn't know.

ESTHER (*she walks*). Yes. That's what I was worried about.

JUDE. Not bad things. Just things. (*He shoots himself with the gun and falls over.*) Did you look after me because you wanted to forgive yourself for something?

ESTHER. You were exciting and unpredictable, a law unto yourself, full of nervous energy.

JUDE (*he sees a Rubik's Cube and picks it up*). Do you remember when I used to do my Christmas shopping here?

ESTHER. It's slipped my mind.

JUDE (*he starts to solve the Cube*). I learned what that something is this morning, it's your need to forgive yourself for incidents that occurred many years ago before I was born, like Derek, like Oliver. I'm not educated, so I've put it clumsily.

ESTHER. It's a conversation we should have another time.

JUDE. It's funny because you say that quite often.

ESTHER. You say you're not educated quite often.

JUDE. I know I've a lot to learn. (*He looks down at the Cube.*) Are you gay, Esther?

ESTHER. Why?

JUDE. I've wondered.

ESTHER. I'm not gay.

JUDE (*he is turning the cube quickly*). You've not had a boyfriend all the years I've known you.

ESTHER. Did you think I might have had a secret girlfriend?

JUDE. No. Yes. I thought it was possible.

ESTHER. I have had a girlfriend once. It was something I tried out. I was very young, and it didn't last many weeks.

JUDE. After Derek?

ESTHER. It was after Oliver.

JUDE (*the Cube is solved. He holds it up*). Did you feel ashamed at the time?

ESTHER. Well done. Ashamed of what, as if I didn't know?

JUDE. Ashamed of being fucked by Derek. I should have asked you about all this ages ago, but maybe it's better left until now.

ESTHER. Every time you say you're not educated I start to worry because I've tried to be a help. I felt ashamed immediately. It was a moment of pure recklessness, but the clock never goes backwards, always forwards. The next day Dolly made her way down the aisle resplendent in a white dress, looking like one of her dolls, in a church filled with people dressed up to the nines. It was her royal wedding. I was culpable, but it took me a while to realise the guilt I was feeling would last forever. The truth nags away, like truth does.

JUDE. You're so funny.

ESTHER. It's made my life very different, Jude, good and bad, who can tell in what ways. If you know guilt, you know how tough life is. I'm not asking for sympathy. I don't feel guilty as a way of forgiving myself. It's moral in all of us to be guilty when we've done wrong. I don't know what an easy life is. I might have hated it if I'd had one. I'm complicated on purpose, it keeps people away. (*She smiles.*) No, I'm not. I'm being silly now. (*She looks at him.*) Derek. I bitterly regret it, Jude. I'm tempted to say the ten minutes I was with him have spoilt my life.

JUDE. You're so funny. He's absolutely a complete cunt. Who else knows?

ESTHER. You're the first. I can't undo what's been said. My world changed this morning. I hope for the better, but we'll see in the future.

JUDE. Your shoulders have dropped.

ESTHER. Have they?

JUDE. An inch. Is it a relief?

ESTHER. Ask me that again tomorrow. I can answer it now, it is a relief.

JUDE. You're funny. You don't cry. I've not seen you cry ever. I used to cry at least once a day.

ESTHER. You didn't to begin with. You were tough as an old shoe. To cry would have been far too vulnerable. Like me, I'm exactly the same. You taught yourself how to cry, like you taught yourself so much.

JUDE. I used to yell and scream blue murder, have a tantrum.

ESTHER. You didn't have tantrums, when you were hot and bothered you hid in cupboards. I should go and catch Dolly. She'll be lost by now.

JUDE. When I was a boy I used to think these pylons said something about the generations, everything gets passed on. You to me, me to my children, should I ever have any.

ESTHER. Catch me up.

JUDE. Yes, I will.

ESTHER. Don't be too long, Jude.

ESTHER *goes.* JUDE *gets his bag and looks out to sea, to the future.*

ACT TWO

A wood on the edge of Tyrifjorden Lake in Norway. Through the trees the fresh water of the land-locked fjord can be glimpsed shimmering like glass in the afternoon sunlight. The large, old trees stretch their branches and cast long shadows on the leaf-mould and dry soil on the forest floor. A fallen log has been sat on many times for many years. A pathway has been trodden through the wood.

JUDE comes one way along the path and ANILA, a girl in her early twenties, comes the other way. They might bump but for JUDE stepping to one side. ANILA walks on and then turns to see that JUDE has stopped.

ANILA. Don't I know you from somewhere, haven't we seen each other somewhere before?

JUDE. I'm looking for Gabriel Twelvetrees. He's an old man. He has a cottage near here by the lake, someplace. He was a famous rock singer back in the day.

ANILA. I know Gabriel Twelvetrees.

A slight pause.

JUDE (*he looks at the bag she is carrying with an Indian motif on the side*). Your bag is a work of art. It's very unusual.

ANILA. I stitched it myself in a few idle moments.

JUDE. This is my first time in Norway, in Tyrifjorden.

ANILA. It's uncanny because you are so, so familiar to me.

JUDE. It's a crazy world, coincidences happen from time to time.

A slight pause.

If I keep on going this way will I come across Gabriel's cottage? I know he likes fishing in the lake with a rod and line.

ANILA. If you keep going, it's not very far. Are you staying in
Vikersund?

JUDE. Yes, I am.

ANILA. At the Tyrifjorden Hotel?

JUDE. Yes, the beds are cosy and comfortable.

ANILA. The older pop fans who want to meet Mr Twelvetrees
often stay there, and the younger rock fans put up a tent.

A slight pause.

JUDE. My Norwegian isn't very good. We did French at school.
I've come all this way and you are English.

ANILA. It's two hours in an aeroplane to Oslo. I've enjoyed
meeting you.

She walks on.

JUDE. I was just thinking we haven't really met properly.

ANILA *stops.*

I live in London. What about you?

ANILA. I'm the same. You are as familiar to me as my own
hand.

JUDE. Where in London exactly?

ANILA. Wimbledon. Wimbledon Village at the top of the hill,
a stone's throw from The Fox and Grapes pub by the
Common.

JUDE. They have very expensive sausage rolls.

ANILA. Where?

JUDE. In The Fox and Grapes. I know every inch of London
and every pub. I used to go to Wimbledon Village on my
bike when I was a kid. I cycled all over London when I was
a boy.

A slight pause.

ANILA. We must have been in the same shop in Wimbledon,
and that's where I saw you. Mr Twelvetrees won't see you.

JUDE. Won't he? Why not?

ANILA. He's a recluse. I'm sorry to be the person with bad news.

JUDE. Are you staying in the Tyrifjorden Hotel?

ANILA. My family rents a house in Tyrifjorden for a month in July every summer and has done since I was a toddler. I must go. My father doesn't like me talking to strange men.

JUDE. We're not strangers if we've met before.

A slight pause.

ANILA. He won't worry for ten minutes. My father is Indian, from Chennai, and he's still overprotective of me and my older brother. He'd sacrifice his life for mine.

JUDE. What does your father do?

ANILA. He's an engineer.

JUDE. I see.

ANILA. He works in the petrochemical industry, one of a small team that designs new plants and directs the building of them around the world, presently he's working in Singapore. He's a clever man. He was the first of only four students to be given a scholarship to Cambridge by the education authority in Chennai. (*She straightens the cloth.*) He likes me to wear a sari some days.

JUDE. You look beautiful, if I may say so, like your bag. I'm very sorry.

ANILA. Why are you sorry?

JUDE. I just am, sometimes I'm apologetic for no reason.

A slight pause.

What does your older brother do?

ANILA. He's followed in my father's footsteps, he's an engineer.

JUDE. What will you be?

ANILA. I'll let you try guessing and tell me.

JUDE. A civil servant, a dentist, another engineer in the family.

ANILA. Touché.

ANILA goes to the log and sits down on one end of it.

It so pleases my father to think of me being an engineer. To me it's so vague, an engineer of what? I've time yet to make up my own mind. I'm at Cambridge doing maths. The university is becoming a tradition, and Indian families know all about tradition, though my mother is English.

A slight pause.

JUDE. You're clever. I'm thick as bricks.

ANILA. Who told you that?

JUDE. I told myself.

ANILA. Poor, poor you.

JUDE goes to the log and sits on the other end of it.

I'm a mathematician when I wish I was brilliant at something else.

JUDE. You can change courses at most universities.

ANILA. Yes, I know.

JUDE. I've a friend who's a teacher. She'd be helpful I think.

ANILA. I shan't tell you what I'd like to be.

JUDE. Why not?

ANILA. You would only laugh.

JUDE. Why would I laugh, is it funny?

ANILA. No.

A slight pause.

I want to be a farmer, with my own farm. Are you surprised?

JUDE. Yes, but it's a brilliant idea. You would look good in wellies.

ANILA. I want to make a difference in the world and I think I could on a farm. I'm making things up even as I have the ideas.

JUDE. I make things up, too, sometimes. It shows initiative.

ANILA. I'm in a real quandary as a matter of fact. I'm tired of numbers. What would you do?

JUDE. I would stop being so serious.

ANILA. Yes.

JUDE. I would smile and have a biscuit.

ANILA. What kind of biscuit?

JUDE. I would try to stop worrying, though I know how hard that is, and let life decide you. There are things in life we can't decide and must decide us.

ANILA. What sort of things?

JUDE. We can't decide who our families are, but we can decide who we love.

A slight pause.

You have come from what is brilliant in the world and I have come from the bad. I've come out of the dirt.

A slight pause.

ANILA. I've never been so undecided. I'm always brim full of confidence. I've had some of the arrogance knocked out of me.

JUDE. Why is that?

ANILA. I like horses. I'd like to plough a field with an old plough and a horse, I think that would be great fun.

JUDE. You should definitely get a horse.

ANILA. I know I'm being silly.

JUDE. You should get two horses and I'll have the other one.

ANILA. I'm not going to be an engineer.

JUDE. Excellent, that's decided, good.

A slight pause.

ANILA. What dirt have you come out of?

JUDE. It's nothing. It was a trivial remark. I was being frivolous.

ANILA. I'm wondering if you were, why don't I believe you?

A slight pause.

I want to understand you now you're becoming a friend.

JUDE. We won't be friends if I tell you. It's nothing. My mother used to hit me and tear at my skin with her nails. It's not important any more. I did think she grew her nails on purpose. It's left me a tiny bit scarred.

A slight pause.

I'm much less scarred than I was once, but it's still hurting.

ANILA. Why did she hit you?

JUDE. It's complicated. It's the most private part of me. It's a long story that I can't really make any shorter, so I'll keep it to myself. One evening she tried to hit me with a hammer, my hands and feet, but I got out of the way. I was in bed asleep and woke up. She thought I was Beelzebub, she thought I was the devil. I could lash out myself, so she might have been right about that. It's all so stupid. It's ridiculous memories that won't go away. Once she tried to push me under the water in the bath and turn on the hot tap, when I was six. She used to put raw potatoes on the table as if it was proper food, a real sit-down dinner. Men would sometimes come in and out of the flat. I'd be given money to go away, a palm full of coins to make myself scarce. I must seem crazy, I know all this is crazy. Sometimes she was a very loving mother, we'd walk along the canal to the zoo at Regent's Park or even go to a gallery to look at an exhibition, she wanted to be a painter, but mostly she was just a fucking mental disease. Heroin had taken away her compassion, it's a drug without any humanity. She was a drug addict, a heroin junkie, so her veins were full of rubbish. Her legs were a map of bruises and ulcers where needles went in and out. It wasn't always her fault when she turned on me, I sometimes gave her back as good as I was given. I used to steal her heroin and sell it. I shouldn't have done that when it made her fuming mad. I came to kind of enjoy it when she was mad. It was a victory.

ANILA. Why was it a victory?

JUDE. I'd won. I wanted to be a winner. If I add two and two I get three, I can't multiply the coefficient by seven, I don't know any of the kings of England, or if water is made up of oxygen and hydrogen, is it?

A slight pause.

I could put her in a spin, send her purple with rage to test how much she loved me.

A slight pause.

I was too busy on my bike to learn much about chemistry and history, bunking off lessons, going to Wimbledon one way and Epping Forest the other. I'd no friends at school. I was the butt of a joke. My best friend was my pedal-bike.

ANILA. Pretending to be stupid can become a vice, like modesty.

JUDE. You remind me of someone else.

ANILA. Someone else who?

JUDE. Esther. She's called Esther.

A slight pause.

I'm explaining some stuff for the first time. I know I'm dreadful and being sorry for myself. Can you forgive me?

ANILA *gets up. She unties a rope and lets down a swing hanging from a high branch. She swings.*

ANILA. My mother is the reverse of your mother. If you were to meet my parents, you'd see how she supports my father, blindly, in everything. His job takes him about the world. She sets up home, takes the same cutlery, in Singapore, in Japan, wherever. He wants a certain pillowcase. It's not for me. In a thousand years, I'm not going to be the little woman sitting politely at home.

A slight pause.

JUDE. Now I think about it, you're sort of familiar to me.

ANILA. I told you we'd met before. I'm always right and never wrong.

JUDE. You're also not afraid of a bold statement. (*He gets up*.) We didn't meet in Wimbledon, I've not been there for many years, and I made it up about the sausage rolls.

    ANILA *stops swinging*.

ANILA. My brother put this up for me a few years ago, when I was too old for a swing. (*There is room for two*.) Sit here.

JUDE. I will in a minute.

    A slight pause.

    I know who you look like.

ANILA. Who?

JUDE. My mother.

ANILA. I don't.

JUDE. You do. I can't explain it. You have something of the look of my mother.

ANILA. What look is that?

JUDE. It's just the way you hold your face. Some memory of her flickers in front of my eyes.

ANILA. I would hate to be your mother, to think of it is like being attacked.

JUDE. I'm sorry, I didn't mean to be cruel that way.

    ANILA *steps off the swing*.

ANILA. I know who you look like. It's suddenly come to me. I don't know why it's taken this long?

JUDE. Who?

ANILA. Gabriel Twelvetrees. You could be Gabriel when he was a young man on *Top of the Pops*. You're the spitting images of one another, the same height and bearing. You're both paper thin. It's quite uncanny.

JUDE. Is it?

ANILA. Yes.

A slight pause.

JUDE. Gabriel is my grandfather.

A slight pause.

ANILA. He's my grandfather too. We're related. We're cousins.

A silence.

JUDE. I think I vaguely knew I had a cousin, now I think. Wow.

ANILA. Two cousins. My brother as well. Two for the price of one. We sort of knew we had a cousin, but there was nothing bad or untoward.

JUDE. Your mother sends me a birthday card every year, and I never reply.

A pause.

ANILA. Grandpa is old. He's a frail old man. All he does is smoke weed all day and go fishing. There's always a smoky white cloud around his cottage. I've just taken him a sandwich for his lunch.

JUDE. Yes.

ANILA. He's smoked weed all his life. In the late 1960s, he went to India with The Beatles and wrote songs with John Lennon on top of a hut, and played the famous, impromptu rock concert on Eel Pie Island with The Rolling Stones. He was a massive man in his day, now he's tiny and mostly forgotten.

JUDE. My mother was coherent, she'd tell me about him.

ANILA. He has ways and means of getting hold of weed. It comes in the post in bags from Oslo.

JUDE. There are ways and means of anything.

A pause.

Does he know about me?

ANILA. I think he does.

JUDE. Will he see me?

ANILA. He must want to see his grandson.

JUDE. Will you take me?

ANILA. What a silly question.

JUDE. Not quite now.

A slight pause.

ANILA. Grandpa is funny. He says he doesn't want company, but he talks ten to the dozen sometimes.

JUDE. What about?

ANILA. About the old days when the pop world was serious, and the music was good, about himself essentially. He's quite selfish.

JUDE. Is he funny?

ANILA. Why?

JUDE. I like people who are funny.

ANILA. Tell me something funny about you.

JUDE. I had a worm as a pet. When he died I buried him in the garden.

ANILA. You're so wonderfully naive and sweet.

JUDE. People thinking that has saved me many times.

A slight pause.

Will you thank your mother for the birthday cards.

ANILA. You can thank her yourself.

JUDE. I'd feel a bit weird doing that.

ANILA. It's going to take a while for all this to sink in.

A pause.

I'm trying to remember what I've said that is too personal and not for family.

JUDE. Yes, I'm thinking exactly the same.

ANILA. We're not friends if we're family.

JUDE. That's a very English thing to say.

ANILA. Is it?

JUDE. Yes.

ANILA. I've always been out on a limb. I always have the feeling I shouldn't be here, I should be somewhere else, doing something different. Everything in my life is in the wrong place.

JUDE. I'm the same. I constantly have the feeling I'm in the wrong body. Wherever I am I'm in the wrong clothes. Perhaps it's in our genes.

ANILA. Yes.

JUDE. I would like to meet Gabriel. I know his father was Viscount somebody or other, which makes our family very hoi polloi. Gabriel went to Harrow. It's always seemed strange to me.

ANILA. Why?

JUDE. I don't know why particularly. I'm not the Harrow boy I would like to be. My skin is public school. I came back to the flat one day and my mother was dead on the kitchen floor, the needle still in the vein in her leg, so there was a small pool of blood with flies in it. It was a few days since I'd been there. I want to ask Gabriel why he didn't care about his daughter and why he let that happen?

ANILA. If you ask him that, he'll shuffle to the kitchen, put the kettle on and make a cup of tea, probably scald himself. You must answer those questions for yourself.

JUDE. Must I?

ANILA. Yes.

A slight pause.

JUDE. How often do you take him a sandwich?

ANILA. Quite often. He's not a big eater.

JUDE. You come for a month every year?

ANILA. In June, July, or August.

JUDE. All the family?

ANILA. Yes, all of us. And my father's mother is here, from India. It's a big house.

JUDE. Grandpa wrote a song about a girl in Paris that was a mega-hit, before he'd been to Paris. I love that. I read somewhere else he came to Norway for the fishing. I'm sure some of it is invented.

A slight pause.

ANILA. He used to want to see a better world, but he won't change. It's beyond him. Change makes him jittery and anxious.

ANILA *sits on the swing.*

Have you been in love?

JUDE (*he thinks*). That's quite a private ask for a cousin. I don't know.

ANILA. You had to think about it, which says the whole shebang.

JUDE. Have you been in love?

ANILA. I might lie.

JUDE. I'll know if you lie.

ANILA. I asked first.

JUDE. No, I haven't. I asked second.

ANILA. No.

A slight pause.

I find my appas's love for me quite difficult.

JUDE. Why?

ANILA. He so wants me to be special, when I want to be a farmer in Wales with a few straggly sheep. He's asked me to meet a boy, and his family in India. A good Hindu boy. He's only nineteen, he's the grandson of his professor in Chennai. He won't mind at all if I say no, but I don't want to let him down. India is not my home.

ANILA *bends down and takes a purse from her bag. She finds a small photograph.* JUDE *goes to the swing and sits beside her.*

JUDE. I've not got an erection. It's just the way my trousers have fallen.

JUDE *straightens his trousers and looks at the photograph.*

He looks nice. He's a handsome boy, I would say. He's an educated face.

ANILA. My appa is proud of me.

JUDE. You're very lucky.

ANILA. I know. Am I? I don't know if I'm lucky. I'll have to educate my father.

JUDE. Yes, you will.

ANILA. My brother won't do that. It's somehow down to me, the girl in the family.

JUDE *gives her the photograph.* ANILA *tears it in half.*

Thank you.

JUDE. What for?

ANILA. Helping to bring me to a decision.

JUDE. It was a fluke if I did.

ANILA. It was no fluke. Where do you live?

JUDE. I have a flat, which I inherited from my mum, in Paddington. I think Gabriel bought it for her, but I'm not there often. Why?

ANILA. I'm looking for a place in London to get away to.

JUDE. It wouldn't be the right place for you.

ANILA. It would only be for a few weeks.

JUDE. You have the best family in the whole wide world.

ANILA. How would you know?

JUDE. I can tell because of you.

ANILA gets off the swing. JUDE takes a small notebook from his bag and writes in it.

ANILA. What are you writing?

JUDE. I write little notes to myself.

ANILA. What about?

JUDE. Just ideas that might be useful one day, thoughts as they crop up.

ANILA. About me?

JUDE puts the notebook in his bag.

About me?

JUDE. Yes. Is that wrong?

ANILA. No. It depends what it was.

A slight pause.

I was asking you to tell me what it was.

JUDE starts to swing.

What was your worm called?

JUDE. William.

ANILA starts to look inside JUDE's bag. JUDE stops swinging.

Please don't do that, it's not yours and there's a loaded mousetrap in there. It will break your fingers into tiny pieces.

ANILA stops. JUDE swings. He swings high. He stops swinging. He gets off.

It's your go.

ANILA sits on the swing. JUDE pushes her.

When we're married, you must let me have a secret bag.

ANILA. Cousins can't marry.

JUDE. We can. Cousins can marry. Most royal dynasties have deemed it essential.

ANILA. There's a boy in Cambridge I've fallen for.

JUDE. Tell me who and I'll murder him.

ANILA. There is no boy in Cambridge for me, in India or anywhere else.

A slight pause.

If my appa wore an apron, I'd have to cut the apron strings.

JUDE. I'll get some scissors and help you.

ANILA. How?

JUDE. I'll put it in my notebook when the how comes to me and let you know.

ANILA. Just now you really alarmed me.

JUDE. Why?

ANILA. You were terribly angry.

JUDE. I'm very sorry.

A slight pause.

ANILA. Would you like to run a farm?

JUDE. I tried wellies once, they were uncomfortable on the top of my foot, like wearing steel. I like gardens, I like plants. I'm not cut out for early mornings and shitty fields. What about you and having children?

ANILA. I would like children, yes, eventually, but not soon.

JUDE. I would love to have children and a family one day if I'm mature enough.

ANILA. I want to live a little first.

A slight pause.

JUDE. You're not a farmer.

ANILA. I keep showing you my ridiculous side.

A slight pause.

JUDE. I just need to grow into myself. I've gone some of the way, but not all the way. A broken child dislikes empty friendships, girls help in just kindly loving me. No one, perhaps, quickly rejects sex, though understandably virgins worry, excepting your zeitgeist.

ANILA. What's that?

JUDE. In the morning, when I was a teenager, I had to think up a sentence beginning with each letter of the alphabet. The talent is leaving me. Once out of bed I had to touch the same twenty-seven items in the same order. That particular craziness has gone. All the rubbish is going out of my life.

ANILA. I like the sentence. Try I–L–Y. Your go.

JUDE. I

ANILA. Love

JUDE. You.

> JUDE *pushes* ANILA *on the swing.*

I shouldn't have said that.

ANILA. It was one simple word. Why not?

JUDE. It's not true. You're funny.

ANILA. Tell me why?

JUDE. You can't possibly know me.

ANILA. I know you get angry if you're afraid. I know you more than you imagine.

JUDE. Do you? I don't think so.

A slight pause.

ANILA. If you were me, what would you do?

JUDE. It's time to please yourself. What makes you happy?

ANILA. Being with you.

JUDE. No, it doesn't.

A slight pause.

ANILA. I don't know about jobs, an engineer, a farmer, a horticulturalist, industrialist, journalist, it's a long alphabet.

JUDE *sits beside her on the swing.*

JUDE. What about Grandpa, have you talked to him?

ANILA. Yes, I've tried to. I tried talking to him an hour ago.

JUDE. Is he wise?

ANILA. Sometimes he can put his finger on a problem. I know pleasing my father doesn't always please me, but I'm hardly unique. He tells me to be more courageous, that life is about courage. I decided when I was five I was good at maths, that was a mistake. Even to admit it to you, takes a little courage.

A slight pause.

JUDE. Is Grandpa clever?

ANILA. He was once. I don't know about now. He lives off the song about the girl in Paris, it buys the weed. Why does it matter so much?

JUDE. I want him to be clever for some reason, I might have inherited some of it.

ANILA. He's old, he's slowed down, you will be disappointed.

JUDE. Is it better not to meet him?

ANILA. I didn't mean that. He's your grandpa. My tatta.

A slight pause.

JUDE. How often have you been to India?

ANILA. We go not quite every year.

JUDE. To your father's family?

ANILA. Yes, or they come here or to Wimbledon.

JUDE. Does Gabriel talk to your Indian grandmother?

ANILA. Yes, his memories of India with John Lennon are very special. It's all he talks about some days. He has albums of photographs, and scrapbooks of memorabilia.

A slight pause.

He has hundreds of books on fishing, and a room stacked high with music magazines.

JUDE. Why aren't you happy?

ANILA. Something inside me is unsettled, like a lot of people. Some of that unsettledness is because I'm clever and won't do as I'm told.

JUDE. Have you ever been to India by yourself?

ANILA. No. I see what you mean.

JUDE. You should. You should see India for yourself. I know London because of a bike. Mahatma Gandhi walked across India to try to understand it. He was a barrister in Temple in London and went home to change a country. One way or another, we all have to grow into ourselves if we're to be any good.

ANILA. Your trousers have fallen in the wrong place again.

JUDE quietly covers himself with his hands.

JUDE. Your father would kill me.

ANILA. He wouldn't.

A slight pause.

You're shy.

JUDE. I just always am.

A slight pause.

It's a big thing for me.

ANILA. What is?

JUDE. Being here with you like this on this swing in Norway.

JUDE lets ANILA take hold of his hand.

ANILA. I look for a four-leafed clover on the Common every spring, to find one makes it a good year.

A slight pause.

I want to ask you a favour.

JUDE. It depends what it is.

ANILA. You have to say yes without knowing.

JUDE. Yes.

ANILA. Will you come to India with me?

JUDE. No.

ANILA. You just said yes.

JUDE. I have to go to America first. I'm a writer, I've got a play going on in New York.

A slight pause.

ANILA. I can't keep up with you. What's the play about?

JUDE. It's about a boy, he comes here to Tyrifjorden Lake to find himself, he meets a girl who he really likes, and they share a kiss, except when I wrote it I didn't know it would really happen.

They kiss, before JUDE *gets off the swing and walks away.*

ANILA. What's the matter?

JUDE. I don't know.

ANILA. What happens in the play?

JUDE. In the last scene he falls in love and opens like a flower.

A woodpecker drums into a tree.

ANILA. Have I done something wrong?

JUDE. I'm worrying you don't really like me.

ANILA. What happens to the boy in the last scene?

JUDE. He weeps as the lights go down, but I'm not going to do that.

A woodpecker drums into a tree.

ANILA. What are you going to do?

JUDE. Go to India with you, but I think some of the time we should be by ourselves.

ANILA. Yes.

JUDE. I think I want to see Rishikesh, in the Himalayan foothills, where Grandpa wrote songs with The Beatles. I won't absolutely know where I want to go until I've talked to him.

A woodpecker drums into a tree.

We should go to Rishikesh together, since he's your tatta as well.

ANILA. Yes.

ANILA gets off the swing and goes to him.

I know I'm too privileged. Can you forgive me?

JUDE. Forgive you for what?

ANILA. My uncertainties.

JUDE. They're quite wonderful, I'll embrace them.

ANILA. It's unusual.

JUDE. What is?

ANILA. To embrace uncertainty. It takes a brave person to do that in a certain world.

ANILA runs her finger under his eye.

You're crying.

JUDE. No, I'm not.

ANILA. Of course, that would be too like the play. It's just one little tear.

JUDE plays his finger across ANILA's lips, and they kiss. They kiss less shyly. ESTHER and DOLLY come on, following the path through the wood. JUDE and ANILA part.

DOLLY (*she comes to a halt*). We've caught up with you at last.

ESTHER comes forward.

JUDE (*he looks at ANILA*). This is the friend I told you about.

ESTHER. I'm Esther. It's very good to meet you.

ACT THREE

The enclosed, shared garden formed by the square of houses at the back of Esther's apartment. Her French windows open onto a small paved area. The building is white, tall and full of windows from the apartments, some lit from inside, others at the top beginning to catch the evening sun. The grass is cut, but not often enough for a perfect lawn, and there are areas of shrubs and some spiky-leafed palms.

Two years have gone by since the time in Norway.

ESTHER is at an old trestle table dealing with many cactus plants. Compost, an old spoon and a washing-up bowl are amongst other the other things filling the table. JUDE comes into the garden. He has a travel bag, which he puts down.

JUDE. You said you'd be in the garden, so I came in the garden way.

ESTHER (*she turns slowly to see him*). I didn't suppose you could grow any more, but I was mistaken.

JUDE. I'm not a child putting on two inches every year.

ESTHER. I don't mean you're taller, I hope it's a few years before I begin to think literally.

JUDE. You look the same, no older.

ESTHER. I'd like to be not quite the same without being older.

JUDE. We'll go clothes shopping. The same Esther who has pots of money and won't spend it until she's made to.

ESTHER. They're gardening clothes. They could go to a charity shop, but charity begins at home.

JUDE. You don't look a day different.

ESTHER. It's seven hundred and ten days since we last saw each other. Knowing you were coming today, I worked it out.
You've been round the world like a member of a boy band.

JUDE. No, not in the slightest like a boy band.

ESTHER. You've a new play coming on.

JUDE. I wrote it in India whilst staying with Anila's grandmother. I sent it to you in one of those old-fashioned things called an envelope.

ESTHER. I thought as plays go it was pretty ordinary.

JUDE. Yes, it's a truly ordinary play.

ESTHER. I've missed you dreadfully.

A pause.

The play is beautiful. It's full of you.

JUDE. Is it? I hate beautiful.

ESTHER. Yes. It brought you back to me as I read it.

A slight pause.

JUDE. I'm sorry I didn't say goodbye, I had to go quickly.

ESTHER. I know, I understood, I wasn't critical.

JUDE. If I could have said a proper goodbye I would have stayed, and I had to go away. It was just the way it was at the time. How are you?

ESTHER. I'm in excellent spirits. I've been doing the garden in Dungeness, taken up the weeds you left behind and replanted some of it. I've tried an apple tree, we'll see. I'm teaching. I've still no idea why some of my students are reading philosophy, but this year they're thought-provoking, in other areas. They're all socialists. It takes me back to my radical time as a student. They came here. I did a Sunday lunchtime roast and they didn't go until after midnight, so I got them taxis home. (*She puts compost into an old washing-up bowl.*) Nobody bothers about the garden any longer. I've been keeping it tidy. The young people who've moved in are too busy at work. (*She adds some cat litter and stirs it with the spoon.*) They want to sit out at the weekend if it's sunny. I've got cactus plants, far too many of them.

JUDE *joins her at the table.*

I'm rather taken up with them. They're going to Dungeness.
I've bought a greenhouse.

JUDE. What can I do to help?

ESTHER (*giving him the bowl*). Stir this with a drop of water, it
doesn't want to be too moist, if the compost looks at the
water that's probably enough.

JUDE (*he adds a drop of water from a small watering can*). Did
you manage to get them to flower?

ESTHER (*she puts on gardening gloves*). I wouldn't want
plants as dangerous as this if they didn't suddenly become
beautiful. (*She carefully takes a cactus from a pot, ready to
repot it.*) I'm learning. They're sharp, even with gloves on.

JUDE. Is that why you've got a box of plasters?

ESTHER (*taking off a glove*). Yes. I'll have one, please.

JUDE (*giving her a plaster*). If you have a newspaper you can
make a noose to help hold them safely.

ESTHER. I've begun reading a newspaper again, and my sister
gets an *Express* when she's here. She's gone off somewhere
today. She's with me so often she's made friends here.

They come to a moment of stillness.

Would you like a cup of tea?

JUDE. No thank you.

ESTHER. I'm happiest being busy doing something.

JUDE. I know.

ESTHER (*she puts the glove back on. She picks up a cactus and
puts the plant on its side, and then uses the end of a
paintbrush to push the plant out of its pot through the
drainage hole.*) I know something has happened, is wrong.
(*She removes old compost from the root ball with her
fingers.*) Some big thing has brought you back from India.
I need a slightly bigger pot than this one, with a little bit of
compost so the plant will sit just below the top.

JUDE *puts compost in the pot and gives it to her.*

Thank you. (*She puts the cactus inside the new pot.*) In days gone by, did you do this with cannabis? (*She puts compost in the pot from the bowl using the spoon and taps the side, so it fills the spaces below.*) Does it seem like a different world to you now?

JUDE. Yes, it does, it's a different world in every possible way.

ESTHER (*she uses the handle of the spoon to push the compost down around the edges of the pot*). A few ideas are going around my head, but they won't be right, I'm not a good guesser.

JUDE *walks away.*

(*She puts a little bit of grit around the top of the pot.*) You're standing where we buried Jeremy, the cat.

JUDE (*he moves away a foot or two*). Am I? It's not fair.

ESTHER. What's not fair.

JUDE. I don't want to burden you.

ESTHER. I want to be burdened.

JUDE. Anila has died.

ESTHER. When?

JUDE. A fortnight ago, in India. She had a heart attack.

ESTHER *throws off her gloves. She goes towards him.* JUDE *walks away.*

ESTHER. Stop. Where are you going?

JUDE *stops.*

JUDE. Nowhere. I had to come home.

ESTHER *takes hold of him.*

She just toppled over in the road.

ESTHER. Were you with her?

JUDE. Yes. I was so inadequate. It was crazy because a young doctor came by. Somehow, we got her to a hospital, but I can't remember much about it now, it's all a blur.

ESTHER. Who was the young doctor?

JUDE. I don't think I knew his name.

ESTHER. Two people could not have done more.

JUDE. Thank you. I was feeling so guilty. Death is horrible.

ESTHER. Unfortunately, it usually is. You don't have to be brave.

JUDE. I want to be brave.

ESTHER. But you don't have to be.

A slight pause.

JUDE. No.

ESTHER. We're allowed to be weak, just every now and again for one minute. (*She holds his head.*) Is it intolerable?

JUDE. At the moment it is. I think we should have had a cup of tea.

ESTHER. Were you in love?

JUDE. Yes, I think so.

ESTHER. You were lucky.

JUDE. Why was I lucky?

ESTHER. Was she in love?

A slight pause.

JUDE. It doesn't feel lucky?

ESTHER. You gave her fun times.

JUDE. I feel so ashamed.

ESTHER. What on earth have you ever done to be ashamed about?

JUDE. I didn't protect her.

ESTHER. She had a heart attack.

JUDE. She was in my care. I suppose we broke the rules. There was a lack of shame about our being in love. We had to be punished.

ESTHER (*she is holding his head*). Would you like me to be clever?

JUDE. Yes, please.

ESTHER. In a moment I'll make an everso intelligent cup of tea.

JUDE. I've been in India, I'm sick of tea.

ESTHER. There is no clever from me. I don't know this, I don't know that, I certainly don't know the other. Don't feel ashamed.

JUDE. I do.

ESTHER. Don't feel ashamed. Feeling ashamed can last a lifetime. Don't feel ashamed. It's not a healthy emotion. Fuck the world, Jude. You must want to fuck the world. You're caring too much, worry less. Don't let the silly people win. Let it all go. Let your history go. Stop living it or you'll end up crippled like me.

JUDE. I wouldn't mind being you.

ESTHER. Thank you.

JUDE. If I could have better clothes.

ESTHER. I bought these clothes last year and I've hardly worn them.

A slight pause.

What about the funeral?

JUDE. It's happened in India.

ESTHER. Anila is there.

JUDE. Yes. In her father's village. I thought it was proper, too.

ESTHER. Will you take me there in a few months?

JUDE. Yes, if you want to go.

ESTHER. I've been envious. (*She whispers.*) Shall I let you into a secret? Dolly is writing her autobiography. She's not told me. I just found a few pages of it. She's using a Biro.

A slight pause.

It's not your fault.

JUDE (*he shrugs*). Isn't it?

ESTHER. Blame yourself when you've been naughty.

JUDE. Naughty? I'm naughty all the time. I used to steal chocolate from the canal-boat café.

ESTHER. I used to watch you do it.

JUDE (*he looks at her quizzically*). Did you know I stole chocolate?

ESTHER. Yes.

JUDE (*he turns away*). I'm quite shocked.

ESTHER. Why?

JUDE. Why didn't you stop me?

ESTHER. You wouldn't have listened.

JUDE. Very, very shocked.

ESTHER. I found a way to pay for the chocolate some of the time. Don't feel ashamed. Don't let it tighten you up. Don't let it ruin you.

JUDE. Yes. (*He goes to the table. He picks up a cactus and puts the plant on its side. He uses the paintbrush to push the plant from the pot through the drainage hole.*) Did I tell you Anila had flu very badly three years ago?

ESTHER (*she has joined him*). No.

JUDE. She was so ill with flu it put her in hospital for a week. (*He takes old compost from the root ball with his fingers.*) The virus attacked her heart muscles.

ESTHER. My gloves are there to be borrowed.

JUDE. I'll risk a scratch. (*He puts the cactus in a new pot.*) The virus stretched and weakened her heart muscles. She died because of flu three years earlier. (*He uses a spoon to put fresh compost down the sides of the pot.*) Anila was sometimes all a dither, she was a ditherer, not knowing what to do for the best. I think being very ill made her that way. It left her uncertain, took away her resolve. (*He taps the side of the pot, so the compost fills the space below.*) She didn't tell me. There was so much we didn't say to each other. Her father told me. He thought she was over the illness. Her family had no idea she was still so poorly. (*He uses the spoon to push the compost down around the edges of the pot.*) Why didn't we talk to each other about this?

ESTHER. She wouldn't want you to be worried. Anila did the worrying for both of you.

JUDE (*he is still for a moment*). Yes.

ESTHER. I don't know why, except saying nothing is easier.

JUDE (*he puts more compost into the top of the pot*). I didn't tell her a hundred things because I wanted her to love me.

ESTHER. You're answering your own question.

JUDE. I think she knew something was wrong in her body from the minute we met in Norway and had tea with Grandpa.

ESTHER. You helped her, let that be enough for you to know.

JUDE (*he puts grit around the top of the pot*). Her heart gave up. Why?

ESTHER. It gave up because she had flu very badly three years ago.

JUDE. Yes. It doesn't make it easier. I'm bruised all over. It's so painful, Esther.

ESTHER. Yes, it will be for a year.

JUDE (*he looks at the newly potted cactus on the table*). I think an apple tree in Dungeness is optimistic.

ESTHER. They said that about putting men on the moon.

JUDE. I'd grow seaweed. You can use it as compost for the cactus.

DOLLY *comes into the garden pushing a wheelbarrow with an oak tree in it.*

ESTHER. Dolly, what are you doing now?

DOLLY. It's a junior oak. A junior oak tree. One day, when we're a few bones in the soil, it will be a grand oak tree. Oak trees are our future.

ESTHER. I don't think I've a pot big enough.

DOLLY. I thought it would be majestic over there.

ESTHER. It's a shared garden.

DOLLY. It's here for one and all to sit beneath the shade of its branches in summer. Do say yes, don't be a fiddly pot.

ESTHER. Yes, why not.

DOLLY (*wheeling the tree to its spot*). The soil will need carefully mulching. When you get the soil right, you get the garden right, Jude knows that. Being a good Girl Guide, I've thought of all eventualities and bought us a spade. (*She comes to a halt.*) You're back from your travels to the five continents.

JUDE. Why does everyone think I've been round the world?

DOLLY. We went to New York to see your play. She cried from the beginning to the end.

ESTHER. I didn't cry.

DOLLY. Yes, you did, enough tears to fill a bucket.

ESTHER. A speck of dust from Manhattan had got in my eye.

DOLLY. We enjoyed it. I didn't know you were so clever. Esther said you would be here this evening. You look different somehow.

JUDE. Do I, for the better or for the worse?

DOLLY. For the worse. She's missed you terribly.

JUDE. I know she has.

DOLLY. For the better. The wheelbarrow wants to go back to Clifton Nursery. (*She starts to lift the tree.*) If I'm dead at the end of this, I'd like 'All Things Bright and Beautiful' sung with gusto at my funeral.

JUDE *goes to help her with the tree.*

There's an oak in York thought to be eight hundred years old.
I sat beneath it a few weeks ago and wondered what it knew.
(*The tree is on the lawn.*) How's Anila?

ESTHER. Anila has died, Dolly.

DOLLY. She's too young, she can't have died.

ESTHER. She had a heart attack in India and died.

DOLLY. You poor child. (*She holds* JUDE's *head and kisses his
forehead.*) Life is always so unfair.

JUDE. How are you, Dolly?

DOLLY. I'm going to church, Jude. I know you don't believe in
God, and I don't think anything of it, but God is looking
after me in these dark times. We went to church as children.
These practices don't go away, they just lie dormant. He will
come to you one day, years from now. You're God's sort of
person.

ESTHER. It's Sunday, Dolly. Don't you want to be getting a
wiggle on if you're going to Evening Prayer?

DOLLY. I've an hour to dig a hole.

ESTHER. If it's going to be here for eight hundred years we
need the right spot.

DOLLY (*standing upright with the spade*). Is this the perfect
place?

ESTHER. No. Move to your left.

DOLLY *moves to her left.*

To your right.

ESTHER *hand-signals and* DOLLY *moves.*

A little bit more. A little bit more. A little bit more. Now to
your left.

DOLLY. You're doing this on purpose.

ESTHER. Perfect.

DOLLY. I'm more or less back where I began. (*She starts to dig
a hole.*) I'll go to Harrogate tomorrow and leave you in
peace for a few days.

ESTHER. You don't have to, Dolly.

DOLLY. Even I find me overbearing, so I do know I'm infuriating. I've a lover to try to find, Jude. Somewhere out there is the special man who doesn't find me irritating. I can't always rely on my sister.

ESTHER. You can if you want to, but not every second.

DOLLY. I feel hysterically randy at times. God tells me it's normal to want a penis and I believe Him.

She digs the hole.

JUDE (*he goes to her*). How are you, Esther?

ESTHER. It's getting to be a frequent question. I'm fine and dandy as I said before.

JUDE. It's frequent because I don't believe the reply.

ESTHER (*she looks at her sister and talks quietly*). There have been some changes, nothing crucial. We'll natter later. (*She starts to repot a cactus.*) There will always be something empty in me. I like the energy that comes from having something missing. If I was satisfied I'd stop thinking, wouldn't I?

JUDE. Yes, I expect so.

ESTHER. Stop worrying.

JUDE (*he helps her with the cactus and talks quietly*). Telling me to stop worrying is like asking me not to breathe. I thought so much while I was away, about you, about the world, about right and wrong. I realised what a moral person you are.

DOLLY. Esther is a Christian, she just doesn't know it.

ESTHER. I am not, thank you very much.

DOLLY. God isn't complicated enough for you. It's about the simple ideas, trust and belief.

ESTHER. I am not a Christian, Dolly.

DOLLY. You need a lover, my darling. The world becomes bearable if we take a lover, I'm presuming. I'm rather hoping. We're born to share our problems, not have them grow larger by being alone.

JUDE. How many cactuses have you got?

ESTHER (*she mimes strangling her sister*). A few, several hundred. I need a Kew Gardens-sized greenhouse.

JUDE. You're being a mite obsessive.

ESTHER. Yes, I know. I'm not particularly bothered, I don't much care.

JUDE. You do really.

ESTHER. What do I really?

JUDE. Care.

ESTHER. The plants fill up an afternoon now and then, like God does for some people. (*She puts her finger to her lips and whispers.*) Sssh. I've found a boyfriend. He's a cactus expert.

JUDE (*he whispers*). What?

ESTHER (*she nods*). Yes. He knows his mammillaria from his echinopsis. Funnily enough, he used to be a gardener at Kew. He's coming here this evening. I'm doing a Sunday roast. Pork and trimmings. He'll be here in a few minutes. He's called Gregory. He doesn't like Greg. He goes for walks along the canal. We passed each other numerous times before we said hello. He said good morning. I pretended to be deaf at first. He smokes, which is not a good thing really. His fingers are nicotine-stained like men years ago. He makes me chuckle. And I think he's probably gay, which is a good thing because I'm not sure if I want to have sex.

DOLLY (*she digs the spade into the soil*). I'm not on the moon, I can hear, I'm not deaf.

JUDE. When I was a boy you used to sit on my bed at night and make up stories.

ESTHER. If I tell it like a story it's because I don't quite believe it's happening. Gregory has asked me to marry him. I've said I'll let him know this evening.

JUDE. Wow.

ESTHER. In an hour or two, I've to decide and know my reply.

JUDE. Wow.

DOLLY (*she stops digging*). Why haven't I met Gregory?

ESTHER. I didn't want you to meet him. We're not in a club that has days out on a bus, we're private.

DOLLY. I agree with Jude. Wow.

A slight pause.

What are you going to reply?

ESTHER. I'm going to say yes, Dolly.

DOLLY. Wow. Wow. Wow.

ESTHER. I've stayed busy whilst you've been at church.

JUDE *walks away.*

Don't go, Jude, where are you going?

JUDE. I don't know where I'm going, I'm going nowhere.

JUDE *stops.*

Gregory?

ESTHER. Yes.

JUDE. I'll fucking call him Greg.

ESTHER. Please don't talk like you're sitting in the gutter, you were brought up to be better than that.

JUDE. How can you be sure you love him?

ESTHER. How could you be sure you loved Anila? I can love, it's not forbidden me, it's allowed, even after all the years of nothing.

JUDE. You had me to support you.

ESTHER. You were a child.

A slight pause.

JUDE. Yes.

ESTHER. You were in and out of my life. I loved you, Jude, until it hurt, but you were a boy, and sometimes I needed a man. You were my child and I thank you.

JUDE. It's not over.

ESTHER. It is.

JUDE. It can't be over.

ESTHER. It can be over. You don't need me any more.

JUDE. I've come back because I need you. This is my place, my home, the garden is mine. What have I done wrong?

A slight pause.

(*He looks down and back up.*) I'm trying to say I love you.

ESTHER. No, you don't, you love yourself.

JUDE. This is absurd.

ESTHER. I've decided to think of me on every occasion, you gave me the idea.

JUDE. And get married?

ESTHER. Probably, perhaps, maybe.

JUDE. I know this is a joke.

ESTHER. Is it?

JUDE. I know it's one of your mad, frivolous japes. A lark.

ESTHER. Is it, are you certain about that?

A slight pause.

JUDE. No, I'm not certain. Why do you want to hurt me?

ESTHER. I don't want to hurt you.

JUDE. You are hurting me. You're doing it deliberately when you know how vulnerable I can be. I want you to tell me why?

ESTHER. This is one of those arguments that has happened by itself. We should stop now, whilst it's still easily forgotten.

DOLLY. In a minute I'll need someone to help me with the compost.

ESTHER. Tip us the wink, we'll be ready. (*She looks at* JUDE.) I'm turning into the woman I didn't want to be and feared becoming. It's hard, Jude, never to have been the most important person in somebody else's life.

JUDE (*he goes towards her*). You're wrong about that.

ESTHER. Am I?

JUDE. By a country mile you're by far the most important person to me.

ESTHER (*she looks at him*). I'm wobbly, like getting on an escalator that's not working.

JUDE. Why?

A slight pause.

I was so nervous a few minutes ago walking into the garden.

ESTHER. You hid it very well.

JUDE. I remember I used to hide fresh bars of soap in your shoes.

ESTHER. Is that the doorbell?

JUDE. I didn't hear anything.

ESTHER. I thought I heard the bell, it might be Gregory.

JUDE. I don't think it was the door.

ESTHER. I'm petrified. I'm shaking inside like a leaf. I wasn't sure who I was going to meet this evening.

JUDE. I've not changed.

ESTHER. But I hope you have.

JUDE. I'm the same person. I'll always be stupid. I learned how to love.

ESTHER. Did you?

JUDE. I learned what love is.

ESTHER (*she looks at him*). I'm jealous of that.

JUDE. Don't you love Gregory?

ESTHER. No. Might I be allowed to pity myself?

JUDE. Yes, sometimes.

ESTHER. The people I've fallen in love with have never loved me.

JUDE. I won't give you any sympathy.

ESTHER. I'd hate that very much.

JUDE. I know.

ESTHER. I've loved quietly or not at all.

JUDE. If it wasn't for me you might have tried harder to meet a bloke.

ESTHER. By the time you came along I was fifty-five, or thereabouts, in dowdy clothes.

DOLLY (*she peers into the hole*). I'm looking at Australia and tipping you the wink.

JUDE (*going to her*). What is there to do?

DOLLY. I haven't said how sorry I am about Anila.

JUDE (*he lifts the large bag of compost out of the wheelbarrow*). You just have.

DOLLY. I didn't say it properly. Daddy died a lot of years before Mummy. His death made me into a more ordinary person. Grief can make us ordinary. It robs us of our sparkle. It would be terrible if it happened to you. Anila loved you because you're nuts. Love is a funny thing, it hurts us when it's not in our lives and hurts us when it is. The compost goes in the hole, you're the expert, I'm just saying the obvious.

ESTHER (*she goes them with scissors*). Scissors might be helpful.

DOLLY. If you cut along the top…

ESTHER. He knows what to do…

DOLLY. There's drawings of scissors and little arrows, if you follow those…

JUDE (*he cuts the bag*). It's compost for idiots.

DOLLY. Gregory works at the garden centre. Is it the same Gregory?

ESTHER. It's a different Gregory.

DOLLY. Garden centre Gregory is nineteen, a student, from St Lucia and wants to be a rapper.

ESTHER. Have you rapped with him?

DOLLY. I'm teaching him everything I know about rapping.

JUDE. How much compost do you want me to use?

DOLLY. I thought you would know.

ESTHER. What did Gregory advise?

DOLLY. He's more rapper than gardener.

ESTHER. The soil struggles with the daffodils, so I would use most of it.

JUDE (*he tips the compost around the hole*). Sydney is wondering why it's snowing compost.

DOLLY. That's not most of it, that's a whole bag…

JUDE. It's unusual compost with a life of its own…

DOLLY. You're being slapdash, Jude.

ESTHER. In eight hundred years the tree will have more on its mind than an inch or two of compost, if it survives the next few hours.

DOLLY. Are we all ready for the big moment?

JUDE. I think so.

DOLLY. I dreamed of this.

ESTHER. You should lift it in, Dolly, it's your tree.

DOLLY. I bought it for you.

JUDE. Why don't I lift it in?

DOLLY. What a sensible idea.

ESTHER. It's like blowing out the candles on a birthday cake, you can make a wish.

JUDE (*he carefully puts the tree in the hole*). That's the wish made.

ESTHER. Is it a tree for Anila?

JUDE (*he picks up the spade and puts soil around the top of the hole*). No. It's for my mother.

ESTHER. Why your mother?

JUDE. I suppose I'm saying goodbye, which I never did.

ESTHER *holds the tree*.

Are you making a wish?

ESTHER. I'm holding the tree for you. And making a wish.

DOLLY (*she treads in the soil*). I've wanted to ruin these shoes, I've never liked them.

JUDE (*he treads in the soil and looks at* ESTHER). What are you wishing?

DOLLY. The tree is not quite straight, my darling.

ESTHER (*holding it straight*). To be graceful when I feel like being poisonous, but I wished for that when I was fifteen.

DOLLY. Can I have a wish?

ESTHER. Yes, why not.

DOLLY. I wish you would stop feeling guilty about Derek.

ESTHER. Is the tree perpendicular?

DOLLY. You're holding it perfectly.

ESTHER. It's a weight off my mind, Dolly.

DOLLY (*she picks up the wheelbarrow*). The wheelbarrow goes back, then to church in these shoes, God is as forgiving as we are.

ESTHER. We'll have the pork after Evensong.

DOLLY. I've ordered a summerhouse which I thought could go over there, to complement the tree.

ESTHER. I do hope you're pulling my leg.

DOLLY. No, I'm serious.

DOLLY *goes off pushing the wheelbarrow.* ESTHER *and* JUDE *are still.*

ESTHER. I'm going to miss her when she's in Harrogate. (*She walks somewhere.*) All bad ideas come to an end. Christianity won't last. It's a religion based on magic. It only works if we believe in miracles. I could argue it. Why don't you take your bag in.

JUDE. I'll see to it shortly.

ESTHER (*she goes to it*). It's only a small bag?

JUDE. It's the bag I took with me when I thought I was going away for two weeks.

JUDE *walks a pace or two.*

Is my room still there?

ESTHER. It's just as you left it. I've not even been in.

JUDE. There's some dirty underpants on the floor I thought you would have washed.

ESTHER. I could carry it in. It's time I put the pork in the oven.

JUDE. How can I help?

ESTHER. You can peel the potatoes, roast, mashed or both. I'm learning how to cook but don't expect genius.

JUDE. What time is Gregory coming?

ESTHER. I don't know if Gregory is coming.

JUDE. Does he live in Little Venice?

ESTHER. He lives in my imagination, which is as good as anywhere.

JUDE. I did wonder if he was one of your jokes.

ESTHER. My jokes, if that's what it is, if it is a joke, always mask the truth. Where boyfriends are concerned I've lived in my imagination. I was happiest there.

The two people are still.

I've cauliflower and broccoli. I know you're not mad on broccoli. I might have a cabbage. Yorkshire puddings in the freezer.

JUDE. It was cauliflower I wasn't mad on but now I like it.

ESTHER. Or carrots out of a tin. You asked me how I was. I don't have pills for breakfast yet. I've not been sunnier than I am at this moment.

The sound of a piano being played drifts into the garden from the top of the house.

JUDE. Is that Buster?

ESTHER. Yes. He plays the piano more and more.

They listen.

I don't know what this is. He's beginning to write music.

JUDE. What are you doing tomorrow?

ESTHER. A group of my students are in London for the summer. (*She begins to move her feet in time to the music.*) We go to the cinema and have a bite to eat afterwards, my treat.

JUDE (*he begins to move his feet in time to the music*). What film are you seeing tomorrow?

ESTHER. It's a surprise every week. They decide the film. What are you doing?

JUDE. I might go for a walk along the canal, through Camden Lock, past Angel and Victoria Park, onto the river at Limehouse and look at the Thames.

They start to dance. ESTHER *holds out her hand and after a moment* JUDE *takes it. Though neither of them can dance particularly well, they begin to pick up on what the other does and enjoy the dance.*

The End.

A Nick Hern Book

The Lodger first published as a paperback original in Great Britain in 2021 by Nick Hern Books Limited, The Glasshouse, 49a Goldhawk Road, London W12 8QP, in association with The Coronet Theatre, London

Cover photograph by Mayumi Hirata

Designed and typeset by Nick Hern Books, London
Printed in Great Britain by Mimeo Ltd, Huntingdon, Cambridgeshire PE29 6XX

A CIP catalogue record for this book is available from the British Library

ISBN   978 1 83904 038 2

www.nickhernbooks.co.uk

facebook.com/nickhernbooks

twitter.com/nickhernbooks